BORDERS REGIO

00083

C000059405

**Also by Joan Woodward**

*Has Your Child Been in Hospital?*

# Understanding Ourselves

## The Uses of Therapy

**Joan Woodward**

**M**
MACMILLAN
EDUCATION

# BORDERS REGIONAL LIBRARY

| ACCESSION No. | CLASS No. |
|---|---|
| R 55235 | 616. 89 |

© Joan Woodward 1988
Introduction © Jean Baker Miller 1988

All rights reserved. No reproduction, copy or transmission
of this publication may be made without written permission.

No paragraph of this publication may be reproduced, copied
or transmitted save with the written permission or in accordance
with the provisions of the Copyright Act 1956 (as amended),
or under the terms of any licence permitting limited copying
issued by the Copyright Licensing Agency, 33–4 Alfred Place,
London WC1E 7DP.

Any person who does any unauthorised act in relation to
this publication may be liable to criminal prosecution and
civil claims for damages.

First published 1988

Published by
MACMILLAN EDUCATION LTD
Houndmills, Basingstoke, Hampshire RG21 2XS
and London
Companies and representatives
throughout the world

Typeset by Wessex Typesetters
(Division of The Eastern Press Ltd)
Frome, Somerset

Printed in Hong Kong

British Library Cataloguing in Publication Data
Woodward, Joan
Understanding ourselves: the uses of
therapy.
1. Psychotherapy
I. Title
616.89′14  RC480
ISBN 0–333–44671–2 (hardcover)
ISBN 0–333–44672–0 (paperback)

To J.B.W.

# Contents

# Introduction

In this book Joan Woodward has accomplished an extraordinary feat. She shows us what really goes on in psychotherapy today – at least with a skilled therapist.

Psychotherapy is about change. It is about people who want desperately to change the parts of their lives that are causing extreme suffering. Equally desperately, they can see no way to change. They have usually tried everything they can imagine to help themselves.

Many people cannot envisage how psychotherapy can enter into such an apparent deadlock and open a path to change. But it can and does. This book shows us how and why.

Joan Woodward's great achievement is making this picture understandable for the 'ordinary person'. As an added bonus, she brings the therapeutic process to life. We can feel the vivid power that attends true psychological change. She shows us both how this change occurs and why the deadlock came about in the first place. These are very complex topics. Many have tried to write about them but very few have been able to illuminate them well, especially without reducing their complexities. Joan Woodward succeeds in this very difficult task. Because she does, the experienced therapist will learn a great deal from her book.

Readers will enjoy this book. That statement may sound strange when talking about serious problems. The enjoyment comes from finding one's deep connections with the truth of people's experience. The book offers a rare opportunity to move along with real people as they make the steps which transform their lives.

In an unusual added feature Joan Woodward asked several of the people with whom she worked to write their stories of their therapy. These accounts provide an important complement to the author's views. They will add to readers' understanding of psychotherapy. Remarkably few therapists have had the courage to put their work to this test. That Joan Woodward did so is further testimony to her deep desire to make psychotherapy understandable. Beyond that desire, her goal is to help to bring the advantages of good psychotherapy to more of the people who can benefit from its particular kind of help.

Most important, Joan Woodward never diminishes or disrespects the people she describes. Instead, she has a deep respect for them and their struggles. She helps us to see that we are all victims of the life conditions which have impinged upon us, but that we can find ways to take action in our own lives. Psychotherapy offers one way in which we can find new paths toward productive action when all the roads had seemed barred.

JEAN BAKER MILLER MD
*Clinical Professor of Psychiatry*
*Boston University School of Medicine*
*Director of Education at the Stone*
*Center for Developmental Services*
*and Studies at Wellesley College*

# Acknowledgements

My thanks go to Vivien Pritchard, who first suggested that I should write this book; to L. Hammer, S. Johnson, H. Meers and A. Young for reading the manuscript in its early stages and making helpful suggestions. Diane Bowen and Lynne Fitton have my thanks for typing and retyping with such patience. I am grateful to Jo Campling, Keith Povey and Victoria Yogman as editor and Steve Kennedy as publisher, as well as Joan Pearce and Terry Fitton for proof-reading. My warmest thanks go to all the clients who have contributed so much to the book, and to my learning. Lastly, I want to thank Jean Baker Miller for being such a source of inspiration to me, and for contributing the introduction.

JOAN WOODWARD

BORDERS
REGIONAL
LIBRARY

# 1 The Purpose of this Book

This book attempts to demystify the processes that occur in psychotherapy. It describes in everyday language the kinds of conflict that drive people to seek therapy. The feelings and processes that people have experienced in therapy as they struggled to gain a better understanding of themselves are shared in detail through the use of many different examples.

For some people psychotherapy is regarded as a rather vague, almost mysterious process. Unfortunately, some books about it make it seem even more so. Many people understandably fear psychotherapy as a potentially alarming process because of the power they feel a therapist may have, either to change a person or to make them dependent. Quite often people who seek psychotherapy feel a sense of shame, that they will be seen as 'weak' or even 'self-indulgent' if they embark on it. Such feelings generally stem from a sense of being 'unworthy' in some way and as such need to be understood, but they miss the main purpose of therapy.

Psychotherapy is a process that enables us to work towards a better understanding of ourselves and the forces that operate both within and outside us in our society, which determine our feelings and behaviour. It is this understanding which plays such a crucial part in enabling people to work towards the sorts of changes *that they want for themselves*.

I believe it to be particularly important for people who work in the so-called 'caring professions', who help other people to develop and change, to have experienced this process of increasing their understanding of themselves. This is because it is a two-way process. Only through working on understanding ourselves can we begin to understand others. Likewise, when we see clearly why

1

someone else feels or behaves as they do, we can sometimes break through some of our own blindness concerning ourselves.

Every day of our lives we are attempting to find solutions to conflicts that arise. Mostly we manage to find acceptable and workable solutions. There are some sorts of conflicts which in this book I define as 'neurotic' ones, when we feel *unable to resolve* deeply torn feelings that arise within us. We are often not aware of the sources of such conflicts. By definition they are the ones that we have attempted to solve by 'neurotic' solutions, although we are mostly unaware that we are doing this. Such solutions tend to recreate the same or similar conflicts over and over again. It is for this reason that some people reach such depths of hopelessness that they may feel that ending their lives is the only way out.

These sorts of conflicts reveal feelings and ways of behaving that generally occur in a number of different aspects of our lives. That is to say, if we think carefully about them we can see that we have had similar feelings in a number of different situations, perhaps at home and work, or within family relationships as well as with friends.

We nearly always know, even if only dimly, that severe conflicts which make us feel torn and helpless and seem so hard to resolve have been very strongly determined and deeply patterned at an early stage of our lives.

Just as we can sense that our inner conflicts started very far back in our own history, so there is a similar sense about the forces at work creating conflict in society. It is not surprising, as Kim Chernin writes (1986), that many young women in the USA feel stuck in certain patterns of behaviour because of their guilt about surpassing their mothers. I believe that these feelings tend to be so severe because of an additional overwhelming sense of their mothers' situation being 'how it has always been'. As Chernin says, new opportunities and expectations for women cannot wipe out generations of traditional attitudes and behaviour.

When we seek to bring about better solutions to conflicts both within ourselves as well as those outside, it is important that we do not underestimate either the complications or the strengths of the forces opposing such changes. We need to give proper recognition to this, and to the length of time it may take some people to discover how to resolve their severe conflicts in new ways.

Perhaps the most important idea to be kept in the forefront of therapy is that conflict, although at times agonising to bear, exists at the heart of all struggle for change. Without conflict and a deep wish to work at understanding the reasons for it, there is no change within us as individuals, nor in society at large. Many conflicts are complicated and difficult to understand at times, because they appear to be made up of paradoxes. That is to say, they are made up of ideas or beliefs which are completely in opposition to each other and yet they are experienced by the same person.

Let us listen to how people actually express some of these feelings:

I *want* to be sexual, but as soon as I know he wants it and he starts to touch me, I freeze up and want to run away.

I so want to be successful, but I feel so inadequate that even if people tell me I'm not, I don't believe them.

I feel *so* hurt and bad when she knows something that I don't; yet what's wrong with not knowing?

I so want to make a loving relationship and yet I feel that if I love someone they will have power over me and I push people off when they get close.

At times these feelings within us can seem so opposed to each other that we feel bewildered and frightened by them. This occurs particularly when the 'split' between the opposing feelings is very obvious to us, and leads to a sense of not knowing fully or properly who one is. So many times people have said to me that they 'don't know which part of them is *real*' – the part that wants so much to do or achieve, or the part that feels so helplessly unable to do it.

I believe that all these conflicting feelings and behaviours, however complicated, are capable of clear description that is both understandable and free of mystery and jargon. For far too long 'experts' have wrapped up knowledge in ways that tend to make people feel ignorant or foolish. This is all part of our hierarchical society, where knowledge is used by some people as a method of maintaining power over others. Unfortunately the field of psychiatry, particularly in the past, has been guilty in this respect. This is largely because it defines and labels people in a very specific way. Once people are labelled as 'sick' or mentally 'ill' it becomes very hard for them both to find and to believe in a different version of themselves.

In this book I have attempted to share some of the unravelling of 'neurotic' conflicts that people have worked on with me, and I have tried to use straightforward language to do so. I believe that everyone can gain from increasing their understanding of their own and other people's feelings and behaviour, and that this applies whether they work with people professionally or not.

If this book helps as a stepping stone to further understanding, especially for people who would not usually read a textbook about neurotic conflict, then it will have achieved its aim.

# 2 Exploring the Beginnings

## The three aspects of mind

Everyone who begins on the voyage of self-discovery soon realises that there seem to be three distinct parts to our minds. One part, of which we quickly become aware, is the part that wishes to 'do', or to 'feel' something. It may be experienced as striving towards a goal that lies ahead. Most commonly it is felt as a longing for a relationship, or for work achievement that feels satisfying and yet seems not available. We become aware of a second part which is often more difficult to recognise as *actually a part of ourselves*. This part seems to be working in opposition to the first part, as if 'it' was determined to prevent 'our' wishes being put into practice! At first it may seem that there are only these two parts 'arguing it out', but in fact there is a third part which is 'aware of' and 'listens to' the other two and which feels separate yet often helpless – either to stop the second part 'sabotaging' the first, or even finding a good compromise between them.

So we listen to the argument in our own and other people's heads:

I wish I could give up smoking – I'm sure I'd be healthier and much better off if I could.

But I'd never keep it up; and anyway if I stopped I'd put on weight.

But if I give it up I'd be able to afford a holiday; that would be nice.

But I'd never cope with work if I couldn't have a smoke; and anyway I'd be impossible to live with.

5

But I really do want to give up; perhaps I'm just too weak-willed! I'll just finish this packet and stop tomorrow . . .

But tomorrow, I've got to face handing in my report . . .

and so it goes on, feeling both interminable and unresolvable.

The example I have chosen is a simple and common one. It presents no conflict for people who have never smoked, for those who have managed to give it up, or for others who smoke and do not wish to stop. However, nearly everyone experiences something about themselves that they want to change yet feel they cannot, and find themselves coping with the conflict by postponing the matter: 'I'll do it tomorrow'.

## Freud's discovery

Freud was the first person to describe separate parts of the mind, giving each part a name. He gave the name 'id' to a part of the mind that he believed had deep hidden aspects to it, and was full of primitive, strong desires which he considered 'instinctive'. The second part of the mind he saw as keeping the first part in order, restraining it and lifting it to higher things. This part he called the 'super ego'.

Most people are aware of this part of themselves, and would describe it as their conscience. However, Freud's view was more complicated as he believed both parts had two different ways of working. One is when we are fully aware of it, and the other when we are not.

The third part of mind that he described was the part that appears to be most logical and reasonable; it is the part we use when we present ourselves to others and feel in control, predictable and consistent. Freud called this the 'ego' (1949). He wrote a great deal about the conflicts that go on between the desires of the 'id' and the restricting 'super ego', and he saw the good functioning of the 'ego' as evidence of some reconciliation of the other two.

Perhaps his translators did Freud something of a disservice in using such strange new words for these parts of our minds, for they are not easy to understand. However, his recognition that by far the largest part of our mind *remains out of awareness* and *yet holds the beliefs that determine so much of our behaviour*, was probably his most profound contribution to contemporary knowledge. I believe it has led to an understanding of our mental life equivalent in magnitude to the understanding of the planet as a sphere and not flat.

## Eric Berne's contribution

Like Freud, Eric Berne was also a psychoanalyst, but he moved away from this way of working. He took Freud's recognition of the three parts of mind, but described them rather differently and in terms that could be far more readily understood (Berne, 1966). He suggested that whichever part of the mind was operating, it affected both how we felt and how we behaved in our relations with others. He describes these as 'transactions' and the understanding of them as 'Transactional Analysis'. He examined in a very detailed way how we relate to each other and the effect this can have. 'T.A.', as it is often called, is now a very well-known method of psychotherapy. Because it is largely to do with relating to people, it is generally carried out in groups.

Berne describes how we can relate as 'child', equivalent to Freud's 'id', or we can relate as 'parent', using the part of us that tries to keep the 'child' in ourselves and others in order. This part is equivalent to Freud's idea of 'super ego'. The third part, able to operate as independent and different, both from the controlling parent and the controlled or rebellious child, Berne described as 'adult', the equivalent of Freud's 'ego'. He made it clear that we move rapidly from one way of relating to another.

Whatever names may be given to these seemingly separate parts of our mind in an attempt to understand how and why we behave as we do, the actual experience for all of us is that we not only 'have' these parts, but we 'are' all these parts in varying ways, with the 'roles' endlessly switching according to whom we are with and the situations we are in.

## Experiencing the three parts of the mind

Most people are able to recognise some occasions when the three parts of their mind are working in opposition to each other. I have chosen to describe two particularly vivid examples when the opposing parts produce conflict within the person. The first occurs when someone feels compelled to turn off taps, close drawers or touch doors in a way that they feel is excessive. Such a person finds themselves caught up in rituals which often become quite complicated and have to be carried out in a particular order. Generally the acts, whatever they may be, have to be carried out a certain number of times. The tap 'must' be wiped three times, or the door re-opened four times; to do it fewer times fills the person with acute anxiety and they feel driven back to do it the 'proper' number of times.

Very mixed feelings are experienced when these so-called 'obsessional' types of behaviour patterns are being carried out. The person is strongly aware of a driving force within, dictating the 'orders' that must be obeyed. They fear that something 'dreadful' will happen if the ritual is not carried out. The harsh and dominating 'parent' from the past is operating within their mind. This may happen regardless of whether the real parent is alive or not. Equally apparent and keenly felt is the frightened, obedient, often exhausted and resentful 'child'. The person carrying out the task finds themselves going later and later to bed, or taking longer to get out of the house, get dressed or to have a bath according to the punishing ritual that they have set up for themselves.

The third part of the mind in these situations is very weak. It is generally experienced only through a rather helpless sense of shame or guilt about the behaviour, and a desire to keep it as hidden as possible. Instead of the 'adult' part feeling strong and able to resist repeating all these acts by either controlling the 'parent' or protecting the 'child', it is experienced as an ineffective observer, bewildered and distressed. This distress is not only due to the painful 'battle' between the harsh 'parent' and exhausted 'child', but also due to the person experiencing their 'adult' part as unbearably helpless. Many people in this situation also suffer increasing criticism, as their family or friends' patience grows thin as they watch the exact folding of garments or the repeated cleaning that apparently must be completed yet again as the person attempts to fend off their intolerable anxiety.

A second example of a situation when the three parts of mind are vividly experienced occurs in people who physically attack themselves. I believe that this behaviour is more common than is generally supposed. It certainly causes very severe distress. The harsh 'parent' part of the person generally sets up tasks or standards of behaviour that seem to the 'child' part of the person impossible to maintain. All manner of 'punishments' get meted out. They may be hair-pulling, angry punching or beating the head with fists or against a wall. Once more the 'adult' part is felt as too weak to intervene, and the person generally ends with bouts of crying and a sense of how 'bad', 'lazy' or 'wicked' they are. They despise themselves and feel helpless as the 'victim' of a brutal attack. Sadly for such a person these behaviours confirm yet again their worst belief that feeling 'good' or even satisfied with themselves is out of reach. Instead a deep and familiar sense of being an unloved failure, known so well from childhood, sweeps over them.

The contented adult is the person who can experience all three parts of the mind, but who has sufficiently reconciled them to each other. Such a person is also able to fit in comfortably with other people's needs to be parent/child/adult in a way that is appropriate.

## Understanding can only be partial

As soon as we start to use ordinary, everyday language to try and describe the experiences we have concerning the working of our mind, we run the risk of being criticised for oversimplifying. In my work as a therapist, however, I find myself in agreement with Malan (1979). He tells us that whenever he thinks he has understood the feelings and behaviour of any of his clients he can be certain that there is always some further complication, another twist or turn left unravelled.

Perhaps we have to be satisfied with knowing that understanding can only ever be partial. For this reason I believe we must be prepared to persevere in the joint task of therapy, to strive to gain at least sufficient understanding for clients to make effective changes in the ways that they wish.

## Recognising effective change

Perhaps the most important aspect of an effective change (in the sense of it being of value to the client) occurs when clients are able to use their increased understanding of themselves and their own needs, to question and challenge some of the attitudes of people around them. It is not enough for therapists just to think in terms of clients' anxiety feelings or depression being lessened, nor merely to increase the clients' tolerance of their current situation.

## Recognising inappropriate feelings

Listening to the changes that clients say they want, and striving to understand the severe anxieties and feelings of sadness or compulsive behaviour that impede their achieving them, it is essential to examine what feels inappropriate to the client in their present situation.

Sometimes this is very straightforward. For example, it does not seem appropriate to Jim, as a healthy young man who works as a salesman, that he should get acute feelings of anxiety associated with sensations that his penis has suddenly become very small, just as he is about to meet a potential buyer. It does not seem appropriate to Jane either, as a healthy young woman, that she feels too frightened to get on a bus to go to work when she enjoys her job. These are examples of 'neurotic conflict' (as defined in Chapter 1). The person experiencing such feelings is bewildered by them and senses that they do not 'belong' to the situations in which they arise.

It is, however, very important that we all strive to differentiate between the feelings that arise from these types of conflicts and those that are 'appropriate', in the sense that they arise as a direct response to an *actual restriction* imposed by one person, or a group of people, on others.

To give just one example – our society is only just beginning to wake up to the frequency with which little girls and young women experience incestuous or other forms of severe sexual oppression. This is mostly, though not invariably, at the hands of men. Many of these girls and women feel both helpless and hopeless about 'telling'. This is because of the burden that the consequences of telling places upon them. Many are threatened with dire punishment if they tell, and they also know that often their stories are unlikely to be believed. They know this because when they start to tell, or to give clues, the message of 'not wanting to hear or know' comes back from others so strongly that no further attempt is made. In any case, even if the story is told and believed, it is highly likely that the suggestion will be raised by somebody that the girl has 'asked for it'.

## How appropriateness is determined

We could stick to a definition of what are 'inappropriate' behaviours or feelings, simply in terms of the distress and pain that they give to the person suffering them. However, I believe it is far more complicated than that, quite apart from the fact that such a definition denies the pain caused by other people's behaviour. There are people whose symptoms and suffering are in fact highly appropriate, in the sense that they are a direct response to their experiences. Such symptoms are often denied or ignored by others, and frequently go unrecognised even by the people who endure them. This is because what is considered 'appropriate' is so frequently defined for people by others.

For generations men have defined to a large extent how women should feel and behave, so that many women have themselves lost the knowledge of what is appropriate. Much of the confusion in women today is due to their struggle to find that out for themselves.

Let us look at one example. For generations, in church ceremonies, at the end of a marriage service the woman is declared 'wife', newly defined only in terms of her relationship to her husband. He remains 'man'. It is only if we reverse them that they seem startling. One wonders what the effect on a congregation would be if the couple were pronounced 'woman' and 'husband'! As this is a wedding ceremony they need only to be defined as husband and wife. Fortunately this is now increasingly occurring, but such definitions are so embedded into our society that I believe many people are only recently recognising their impact on the way we think about ourselves.

These types of definitions, that imply ownership and property, can have very profound effects on our beliefs about what is, or is not, appropriate behaviour.

Just as men have very largely had the power to define and, therefore, determine how women should be, so adults do this to children. It is much easier to determine children's behaviour, as this can be done from the powerful base of adult knowledge and under the guise of benevolence. Occasionally, however, an exceptional adult like James Robertson, making a film of *A Two Year Old Goes to Hospital* (1952), compels others to witness how it actually *feels* to a small child to be separated from parents by a hospital stay. This film helped to explode the myth, held so strongly at the time, that small children 'settle down' in hospital and do not need their parents. In fact the cries and sobs from small patients were often seen not only as 'inappropriate behaviour' (after all the child was there to 'get better' and the nurses were kind), but paradoxically the children's crying at visiting time actually tended to make hospital staff *limit* parental visiting even further.

The fact of being oppressed, in the sense of having one's lifestyle largely determined by others, is the very factor that has rendered both women and children's views to be so readily discounted. This also applies of course to other groups such as the handicapped, the elderly and perhaps above all, to black people living in a white society. So often in the past when women have tried to make changes for themselves the charge they have had to meet is that of being 'unwomanly'.

As a research investigation in the USA suggests that therapists are not free of sexist views (see I. and D. Broverman et al., 1970, pp. 1–7), it seems very important that all therapists make a particular effort to remain as open-minded as possible. They should listen to people's views of their inner discomforts, and try to hear them with clarity, and not in terms of a prescribed or stereotype viewpoint. Above all, they should listen to their clients' *actual experiences*.

A woman once described to me her deep sense of worthlessness. She was the second girl in her family where the first child, a son, had died soon after his birth. She experienced herself as her parents' 'failure' to replace the longed-for son in a society which traditionally gives enormous value to the son who carries on the family name. Her 'neurotic solution' to the unbearable conflict arising from being viewed as having the 'wrong' gender was to hide herself away, and show herself only in ways others might want her to be. She was an extreme example of what many little girls experience, in feeling a deep need to please in order to gain approval in a society where this is demanded from girls. As she grew older, her own *real* feelings and needs became more and more denied. She sought therapy because acute anxiety arose when she tried to have her first sexual relationship.

It is especially important first to acknowledge the clients' view of what feels appropriate to them, and for the therapist to make sure that they do not misread 'symptoms' caused by the deeply oppressive aspects of life that many people endure, but sometimes fail to recognise even for themselves.

**Writing about theories**

So much has been written concerning the theories of human behaviour and about therapy, but much of this concerns diagnosis and classification of symptoms. Surprisingly little seems to have been written about the experience of therapy; how it is carried out and above all how changes in feelings and behaviour actually occur.

I believe it is this lack of information that makes many people think that psychotherapy is some little-known, mysterious process. In fact it is nothing of the kind. We are all continually confronting the very basic question of how, as individuals, we can use our understanding of ourselves to move away from ways of behaving that we dislike and from which we wish to free ourselves and move towards less distressing ones. Sometimes feelings or ways of behaving are experienced as driving us so compulsively that we can feel trapped and quite unable to see any way out of them at all. This is particularly true for anybody with very strong, deep-rooted fears.

In the chapters that follow we will examine the reasons why people feel driven to behave in ways that give themselves and others distress, and how changes can be made when people really want to make them. It is important to move slowly and carefully through the 'mazes' that others have experienced as they have sought to understand themselves, and questions must be asked at each twist and turn in order to catch and recognise the statements that may appear like 'throw away lines' but which hold great significance for the person. I believe that all feelings and behaviour make 'sense', and can be understood, provided *both* the actual experiences and the resulting beliefs that have been formed are examined carefully. In this way the beliefs that people hold about themselves are recognised as having come out of actual experiences – the loss of a parent, their place in the family or their parents' attitude towards them.

In a recent research study that I undertook into the effect on bereaved twins of the loss of their twin, the attitudes of their parents were found to be of profound importance (see Woodward, 1987). Some of the higher levels of emotional distress were found in the adult twins, who believed that they were the ones their parents wished had died rather than their twin.

Some of the parents might be able to admit this was so. Others might strenuously deny it. What is important is to appreciate that it was the twins' *belief* about their parents' view that caused them pain and damage.

When listening to clients' accounts of their feelings and how they experience events in their lives, it can feel rather like being engrossed in a film, as one listens to the account being unfolded. In the cinema, watching with a 'real' film, I often wish I could stop it or run it back to a previous point to make sure I have seen all the connections. In therapy one is actually able to do this! In fact I think it is essential at times to stop a client, to 'hold the film', and say, 'Let's play that bit through again, very slowly and try to share a fuller understanding of what's in it'.

### Understanding is only part of the therapy

Striving to understand feelings and behaviour within the context of the person's actual experiences is, I believe, an essential part of therapy. But it is only part of the work involved. Sometimes people understand very well how they have come to feel and behave as they do. In order to change they also need to express and share the deep pain, sadness or anger involved in letting go of their old ways of being. They also need to find a deep wish to move towards new ways. Only then can their understanding be used as part of the means to obtain a change. Changes come only when certain beliefs are let go, and such beliefs need in the first place to give us considerable discomfort before we will even examine them, let alone consider therapy. How easy we all feel it would be to achieve certain goals if *only* we did not 'feel afraid' or 'lack confidence' or whatever the barrier is perceived to be. The fact is, however, that we have to tackle the goal *in spite of* the fear, sadness or inadequacy that grips us.

Jim, for example, feels that 'if only' his penis didn't seem to shrivel up he could walk into the biggest firm and confront his buyers with ease. Jane, too, feels that 'if only' she had the confidence, how easy it would be to get on the bus. But much as we wish they would, those sort of fears do not go away *first*, leaving us free to do the things we want to do. We actually have to find ways to *start to do them*, in order to make the fear go away. It is this very 'Catch 22' sensation of the vicious circle that seems so hard to break.

These ways of thinking are not limited to feeling afraid of things we want to do. They are also present very strongly in beliefs we may hold about ourselves – for example, that we feel ugly, or unattractive, that nobody likes us, or that we cannot make friends.

For most people, once they recognise and really understand for themselves that the cause of these feelings originated from real experiences that happened in the past, they see how the pattern was set and how beliefs have built up. So it becomes clear that we all continue to behave as if we were facing the same situations in the present. Jim creates the sensation of the tiny penis of the small boy whenever he confronts a potentially threatening father figure. Jane feels that going on a bus awakens sensations that something dreadful will happen. It is as if going off into the wide world was both an abandoning and a destruction of her family, which is her own secure base.

As recognition of where these feelings started and how they built up becomes clearer, so their present inappropriateness becomes more obvious. The purpose for them that once existed does so no longer, and it is the recognition of this that forms the first step in enabling the person to experiment in letting them go. Some people imagine that deep traumatic experiences must lie at the back of such fearful patterns. This is not necessarily so. The parental attitude to the place one has in the family, as first born, or only child, can be the basis for perceptions about oneself that cause ways of behaviour that can last a lifetime.

Kovel (1976) accurately describes how breaking free of neurotic conflict does not feel like leaping out into freedom or light.

In fact, it is often experienced as a huge struggle, sometimes accompanied by a great sense of loss. As he says, we all howl all the way!

## Distress from conflict drives people to seek therapy

For many people anxieties or feelings of depression have to be really severe before they are motivated enough to examine their causes and try to unravel the maze. I think this is because most of us fear change, and 'the devil we know' is better than the 'devil we don't'! In other words, we may prefer to put up with ourselves as we are, rather than embark on examining our feelings in case we find something more alarming in the process. Many people fear that if they delve deeper into themselves they will find inner feelings that will overwhelm them, or meet aspects of themselves that they will hate on discovery.

This way of thinking is an example of a protective device that *maintains* our way of feeling and behaving, as it prevents it being exposed to the light of day. In other words, we say 'Don't look – it could be worse', and this guarantees that our beliefs and feelings remain unchanged. In this way we use our imagined fear that a change will be for the worse, to stop us having the opportunity to change for the better.

Some people request therapy with no intention of changing at all. In fact occasionally their main aim seems to be to prove that change is impossible. Whatever their degree of suffering it seems most likely that such people are exceptionally frightened of change. I believe that this deep fear of change needs to be recognised at the very early stages of therapy. Such people need extra time and encouragement to examine slowly and carefully the nature of the deep sense of loss that they fear will be involved in changing themselves.

If this sort of gentle exploration is not done the old ways of behaving, and the beliefs that underly them, simply become stronger as they begin to be challenged. This seems to occur regardless of how much discomfort certain ways of behaving may produce for the person concerned.

An example of this arose in a man who had beaten up his wife and later another woman he lived with. He always suffered great

feelings of remorse and shame afterwards. The physical attacks
always occurred because of his acute sense of frustration, due to
the woman he was with not 'seeing' that *his* advice or way of doing
something was 'right'. If she criticised, or ceased to be grateful or
appreciative, or wished to do something differently, he became
very distressed and angry. His belief in himself as 'knowing best',
in providing something 'wonderful' was strongly challenged. He
found it impossible to look at the fact that his way of behaving
actually deprived the women he lived with from having the very
'right' that he demanded for himself. He saw no solution in
compromise, for he perceived his way as 'best' and found it hard
to understand why others could not accept it. He wept from
feelings of being unappreciated, not only at home but also at work.
He sought a therapist who would confirm his 'rightness' and
support his view of how 'wrong' everyone else was in failing to
appreciate the expertise he had to offer. He could see, in theory,
that gifts and advice can only be fully appreciated if they are in
the form that the receiver wants them to be, but for him to carry
this out in practice would have meant letting go some of the power
to control other people's lives, which he felt unable to do. He was
determined to make people at work, 'pay' for having opposed him
and yet such vengeance did not make him happy.

I believe most emphatically that the wish to change and the
speed of work must always be determined by the client. For
therapists to impose their wishes in either of these spheres is
inexcusable.

# 3  The Experience of Conflict

In this chapter we hear how a number of different people feel when they are experiencing conflict due to different parts of their mind working strongly in opposition to each other. We also hear what they can learn about themselves during therapy. Each of the stories that follow illustrates the person's sense of being torn between how they want to be, and wish so much they could be, and yet how driven they feel to be the opposite.

How these conflicting feelings have come about gradually becomes understood as the person recognises the beliefs that they hold about themselves. These come from their early life experiences even though, as Alice Miller describes (1987), there may be no clear memory of them. The responses that they have created, however, are strongly felt in the present. These are generally experienced in the form of the person feeling consistently 'bad' or 'guilty' or unable to accept ordinary, good feelings about themselves. As therapy proceeds, the client and therapist share recognition of the 'neurotic solutions' that the client has felt compelled to put into effect, but which have failed to resolve the conflict for them.

It is interesting to recognise that in every case it is the *failure* of these 'neurotic solutions', and the pain that they cause by their ever increasing inappropriateness, that drive people to seek therapy and to find some answers to the question: 'Why do I feel like this?'

### Keeping people alive

When Margaret first came to talk to me she was aware of her huge need to look after everyone; her husband and children in particular,

18

but also other family members, her friends and neighbours and all
the students in the classes she ran at Evening School. This 'looking
after' took many forms. If a distressed neighbour called, however
inconveniently, to request baby-minding or a loan of something,
or a chance to pour out their woes, Margaret felt she must never
say 'no'. If asked for advice she would get a book on the subject
for the person to read. She would then feel obliged to take it
round. She felt she must cook food for people, invite the family
to stay; always *she* must do the caring.

On the other side of the 'good fairy', vision of herself was the
person she described as the 'bad fairy', who raged and screamed
and wept and felt resentful about all the demands that everyone
seemed to make on her, which not only overwhelmed her, but
also left her feeling she could *never express any needs of her own*.
As she spoke of these feelings she became deeply distressed at her
own sense of unworthiness.

The more Margaret talked, the more she became aware of the
compulsive aspect of her need to care for others, with a lot of
anxiety created for herself if she failed to do it to the full. It was
becoming such a burden that when she sought therapy she was on
the point of giving up her Evening Classes, because she felt she
was not giving sufficient care to her students. The immediate
'trigger point' came when a close neighbour with a small baby
suddenly widowed, and started making huge demands for her
support.

Margaret soon began to recognise that at times she felt that if
she did not give the right sort of care to someone she would
actually feel responsible for the person dying. She spoke of how
she had felt afraid to tell her son to go somewhere on his bicycle,
for if he should get knocked down she would feel responsible.
Alongside this, she feared her husband might leave her, and felt
acutely jealous of his interest in any women he befriended. I find
it hard to accept the traditional psychoanalytical view that there
must be deep wishes, operating at levels of which Margaret is
unaware, that in some way she wanted the death of her son or
husband. I think we need to stick hard to the evidence she provided
of her own experiences and the beliefs that came from it. It seemed
as if she expected and deeply feared the loss of the men she loved,
and that she felt that her own 'unworthiness' made her doomed
to have this happen. Worst of all she feared that her very desires

and deep need for their love might inadvertently bring about such a loss.

Margaret's conflict was clear; she was feeling and behaving as if she was the sole life support system for everyone, as if she *had* to give constant caring to keep people alive. If she failed they would or could die, as she alone had not only the power to keep them alive but a driving responsibility to do so. The burden of all this felt so massive that it often exhausted her, and at times felt quite unbearable.

I accept John Bowlby's view (1980) that these beliefs arise from perceptions formed out of real experience. I listened to Margaret's history to discover with her when it all began. She and her brother had a loving, fairly ordinary early upbringing, until as a schoolgirl she became very keen on going to the cinema. The family was hard up, and films were a special treat. On one occasion when there was a 'flu epidemic, Margaret wanted very specially to see a film. She begged her father, whom she loved dearly, to take her. Her mother said no, it was too dangerous to go to a crowded place as they would catch 'flu and die. Margaret persisted and her father took her. Later he developed 'flu and he died. Almost immediately their entire lifestyle changed. They moved to a very restrictive and gloomy house of some elderly aunts. Their mother had to go to work, and Margaret's brother made it clear that he considered the entire disaster her fault. No doubt there were many complicated twists and turns in Margaret's feelings and fears, but uppermost was the actual experience that made her believe that her desire to have something special with her much-loved father, chosen in defiance of her mother, had led to his death. The belief that she was indeed the 'bad fairy' whose 'wants' had killed her father and ruined the lives of her mother and brother left her believing that her wishes had led to his death. Her only 'solution' was to make sure that she never asked or chose anything more for herself, and that she worked hard to keep everyone alive, to avoid any repetition of such 'destructive powers' ever occurring again.

At one stage she laughed, as she said how often her family commented that she could never decide to have anything for herself. Even at the family supper table they said 'Mum, you go first' when there were pots of different yoghurts to choose from. She could not; she always had the one at the end, after everyone else had chosen. Her wishes could not be expressed, even for a yoghurt.

## The compulsive need to care

Rosemary was another person feeling compelled to care. She came for therapy requesting to work on her deeply distressed feelings about being let down by a man she had loved very dearly. He had been giving her 'double messages', showing her that he loved her and that she was very important to him. Then he would let her know of his continuing obsession with a previous girlfriend. This would be followed by remorse and further vows of love from him. This reached a peak when he asked her to marry him, and on the morning after she had agreed he suddenly told her that he had made love to his previous girlfriend only three nights before and was missing her very much. At that point Rosemary felt near to breaking. She left him, her home and her work and returned to her parents. She realised that promises of love followed so rapidly by denials terrified her, and the frequent nightmares she was having showed her fears of 'going mad'. Gradually she realised that she was someone whose standard of loving and staying within a relationship actually increased the greater the hardship or rejection she endured. She was operating like some of the women Robin Norwood describes in her book *Women Who Love Too Much* (1986). Rosemary realised that she had similar feelings towards her elderly parents. She went to enormous lengths worrying about them, driving herself to be with them and care for them. Her awareness of this arose in a startling way when her father complained that she 'over-mothered' them. She realised that she felt equally driven to give her all to her work, often staying on to finish tasks until late at night so that more and more became expected of her. As she realised how unstintingly she gave loving and caring to others, so she saw how very little love and care she gave herself.

When she started to examine when this pattern of behaving began, she recalled a time that stood out very strongly in her memory. Her father was frequently verbally abusive to her mother, and Rosemary recalled often feeling very frightened and helpless watching this behaviour and begging them to stop rowing. On one occasion, around the time she was about six years old, she remembered her mother being so badly beaten about the head that she got into Rosemary's bed with her. She remembers holding her mother's head and 'trying to nurse it better'. She never saw any affection between her parents, and as she recalled all this she saw that she had taken on the task of 'making it better' for the world. The harder it was to do, the more she worked at proving she could do it. She felt she was to *blame* for her mother's trapped situation. Her mother had told Rosemary that 'if it wasn't for you children I would leave'. Rosemary took on the responsibility for 'putting it right' and continually gave to others the loving care she never had, that she so badly needed for herself, but felt compelled to give away.

This compulsive need to care is one of the commonest 'neurotic solutions' and is displayed far more often by women than men. This is because it is far more usual for strong pressures to be put on females, starting when they are small girls, to meet other peoples' needs in preference to their own. Women like Rosemary have often witnessed violence between their parents and suffered from lack of love for themselves. As they *give out* the very love they so want in order to believe in their own value and goodness, so they feel more and more 'empty' inside themselves. Their desperation increases as their 'neurotic solution' fails to supply their needs.

**'No space'**

Jean, born of elderly parents with much older siblings, expressed feelings that she 'could never win'. It felt to her as if there was 'no space' for her; however hard she tried to make a place for herself it was never really there. As she spoke of this intolerable conflict – her absolute need to find a space for herself and yet her belief that it did not exist – she began to recount her history. Her mother, worn out with childbearing and the loss of three children born previously, had understandably little enthusiasm or energy left for her unplanned sixth child. Jean described how as a little girl she had to behave perfectly as she accompanied her mother to work.

Her early experience of having no space for herself occurred when she slept in a cot in her parent's bedroom until she was five, and her feet 'hung over at the end'. Later, with her older sister reluctant to share her bed, Jean found a space for herself on summer nights in a bed of her own in the cycle shed. Much later as a student she would return from her vacations, only to find rooms in her home let out to boarders to increase the family income. Jean had to bed down with neighbours.

As an adult Jean faced two severe losses. Her boyfriend died and an important job came to an abrupt and unexpected end. Jean's 'solution' to the pain of finding 'no space' available for her was to withdraw; to cease searching for it and no longer to believe in its existence. She drank heavily, sat inert for hours on end, and at her worst moments contemplated suicide.

A good deal later she came seeking therapy at a point when she had started to change her career. Partly because of the 'withdrawing' (the inertia and drinking) she had failed an essential examination and was contemplating a 're-sit'. This was yet another direct confrontation with the conflict. She *wanted* to pass the examination and have the work it would bring, but she had the gravest doubts whether it could really be hers. At this stage she felt unable to clean the house, or make use of her garden, and even contacting friends was very difficult.

To label such a person an 'alcoholic' gives little clue about effective help and in some sense it represented to Jean the very cul-de-sac she felt herself to be in. Her conflict was experienced as being about a deep wish to get what she really wanted for herself, but as soon as she attempted to reach out for it she felt it was taken away. Suddenly, there was 'nothing there'. She was vaguely aware that the 'solution' to withdraw and to drink in order to protect herself from the pain and terror of finding 'nothing' actually played a part in guaranteeing there would be 'nothing'. As the time for the 're-sit' of the examination drew nearer, so the drinking got heavier, and she became more engaged in 'sabotaging' her chances of getting what she wanted. This was not because she did not want it, but because of a deep fear that if she had it it would be 'taken away' once again.

For Jennifer there was a different variation of these 'no space for her' feelings. She was the second of seven girls and had always had to share her mother with her many sisters. When she sought therapy she had recently finished her studies at Art College. She felt isolated from friends and spent a lot of her day lying around in her bedsitter, very distressed that she could not finish the art work she so wanted to do. Her strong negative views about herself and her dreadful sense of failure drove her sometimes to hurt herself, often beating her head against the wall.

The more Jennifer talked about her feelings, the clearer her conflict became. She believed that whatever she wanted she could only have at 'someone else's expense', as this had been her family experience. If she successfully completed a picture other people would be jealous of it. Her 'gain' would be perceived as their 'loss', and she would be hated for it, just as she had always felt herself to be as a child when there was competition for her mother's love. With her family and her friends she felt that either they were always asking 'too much of her' (she would have to be the endless supporter, doing things their way, comforting and nurturing them) or, as the other side of the same coin, if she dared to ask for anything for herself she would be perceived as the devouring, demanding person who would inevitably be rejected as greedy and insatiable.

She had many memories of wanting her mother's love and attention, and of her mother being 'too busy' and 'too tired' with yet another pregnancy or small baby to look after, to give Jennifer the love and attention she wanted so much. Her mother had died shortly before Jennifer sought therapy. She believed that her mother's death was due to her being worn out from trying to care for them all and to meet all their demands. The 'solution' for Jennifer was to demand nothing, to become self-sufficient and not to achieve or have anything for herself. Yet this too was unbearable in its emptiness and its isolation. With no creative achievements, no special relationship and separated from her family, she realised that the 'solution' of 'moving away' and denying her needs had failed to bring the reward of the love and approval she so desperately sought, that it had been originally set up to achieve.

## Fear of being successful

Joyce presented her conflicting feelings in terms of perceiving herself as 'inadequate' and a failure. Yet to live with such a view of herself was intolerable. Her marriage had broken down, so she felt a 'failure' as a wife. She felt 'no good as a mother', as she struggled to manage her two small girls largely on her own. She felt quite incapable of doing a job. She said her marriage had actually failed because she was so 'inadequate'. What was more, whatever anyone said to the contrary would make no difference because she just would not believe them. So she defined herself as a 'failure' and saw no way out – yet she hated it. Why did being a 'failure' have such a determined ring to it, and why had she shut the door so hard on even hearing *anything* to the contrary?

The question inside this very painful conflict seemed to be: why did Joyce feel it was so *risky* to be successful? Her story came quickly. As the only girl in her working-class family, Joyce had had a loving upbringing even though it had been very restrictive. She did well at school and her teachers insisted she should continue to 'A Level' and university. The response from her parents, however, was strongly negative. At the time she was not able to explain to her parents her wish to continue at school and university. Her brothers had already left to do other things. She felt upset, confused and frightened as these wishes to go on to university were seen by her parents as their daughter launching into a world that they knew nothing about. Her need to separate successfully and to explore academic work conflicted with her parents' wish to have her living at home. They imagined her working locally, living very close and playing a continuing part in their life.

For Joyce to leave home, to launch into university life, was equivalent to abandoning her parents. For her to grow and to succeed would mean not only facing a deep sense of guilt, but also to lose, as she perceived it, her parents' love and approval. Without these she felt unsure whether she could face the challenge of the university world. For her parents it was a world so unknown to them, and they saw it as making a very deep separation. The 'neurotic solution' for Joyce was to make sure she never succeeded at anything, for to do so was far too risky.

Rita had a similar conflict. She came from a family with very strong religious convictions. When Rita started a sexual relationship with a fellow student she felt unable to continue with it, having to keep it secret because of her parents' strong disapproval. Her response was to lose all her sexual desires. Both these women had in common the same 'neurotic solution' – to 'fail', to 'block off' any deep desires to 'succeed' in areas that caused such conflict for them. Such a solution ultimately produced severe distress for both of them.

Rebecca had a different version of feeling that 'success was dangerous' for her. She had a mother who was the exact opposite to Joyce's. Rebecca's mother was a successful woman, active in public life, who was frequently away from home. Rebecca's main memory of how she felt about her mother as a child was a mixture of longing for her love but at times feeling that she could never compete with her, but also deeply seeking her approval.

When Rebecca started therapy she had produced a son. This had followed a very distressing period when she had had a miscarriage. She had a daughter, but had a great fear she would not be able to have a second child. Many of her friends were pregnant at the time and she felt painfully jealous of them.

When her son was born she felt particularly proud of him. He was a very beautiful child and she named him after both her husband and her father (who had died less than a year earlier), giving the boy a rather unusual composite name.

This was followed by Rebecca experiencing the most intense sense of failure. She spent many hours thinking about her son's name, talking about it and feeling it was not only a source of embarrassment but also 'evidence' that she could not even choose an 'acceptable' name for her own son. She feared that she would be ridiculed and rejected because of it. In this way she attempted to turn the 'success' of bearing her son into what felt like a devastating 'failure'. By giving her son no name for himself that was just his own she had succeeded, in a sense, in denying his existence. Her fears about her deep feelings towards her father became clear as she spoke of the closeness of the date between her father's death and the conception of her son. She was able to perpetuate her father's memory by having given his name to her son.

Rebecca had never felt able to rejoice in her achievements with confidence, and the arrival of a deeply longed-for son set up such conflict that she had both to deny his existence and punish herself in a way that prevented her from enjoying him. Obsessional thinking patterns revolved around her choice of his name, which kept both her and her husband awake into the small hours for very many nights. She experienced these as a very distressing torture.

Much later she recognised that the many occasions when she had behaved as if her son did not exist gave her a sense of sadness, because she had had so little pleasure from his early life.

Rebecca's mother had already shown some anxiety over losing closeness with Rebecca through her marriage, and had expressed competitive feelings towards Rebecca's husband. The arrival of Rebecca's son, so close to her mother's loss of a husband, increased the need for Rebecca to deny her achievement.

## Compulsive fear of 'being a baby'

One of the most common conflicts experienced by girls who are in reality very competent and generally the youngest in their family, centres around being desperately afraid that they cannot control wetting or soiling themselves in public.

This fear seems to arise most frequently at secondary school age or at an early stage of being a student at university or college. The fear of wetting or having diarrhoea makes them feel that they cannot stay in the classroom or lecture room and develops into severely restrictive sensations, as it makes travelling so fraught and visiting anywhere new utterly impossible if the whereabouts of lavatories is unknown.

Rushing out from a class to a lavatory attracts attention and causes embarrassment. It also brings mounting pressure for an 'explanation'. The fear that they will be overcome and wet or dirty themselves in public is often accompanied by vivid fantasies of how they would feel if this occurred. In fact, it is very rare for it to happen in reality.

The idea of 'wetting' represents total humiliation, a final exposure of their own inability to control themselves. They fear it will lead to their being ridiculed and rejected, and regarded as the 'helpless baby'.

Christine, who felt so perturbed about her fear of wetting that her parents were prepared to take her out of school, saw that the conflict around her apparent 'need' to be this 'baby person' was so strong that she feared she would not be able to control it. She hated it very much and recognised its apparent 'inappropriateness' to an agonising degree.

What was Christine attempting to solve, if she so hated being like this? Why was she doing it? What purpose did it serve? She recognised quite quickly that it was about keeping her parents' concern and attention, as well as assuring her a sheltered, protected position. It also stopped her from being the 'successful' schoolchild, like her older sisters, both of whom had achieved the highest possible honours. She was able to acknowledge with a grin and a sense of relief that being a 'baby' had also hidden a wish to 'piss all over' some of her contemporaries at school, whom she viewed at this stage as a 'stuck up lot'. This also aroused very similar feelings to those she had felt towards her brilliant sisters, both of whom had scorned her many times.

Alice carried a bottle of kaolin medicine around with her whenever she left the house, which she had great difficulty in doing as she was afraid of being struck by an attack of diarrhoea. She very much wanted to continue with her course at college, yet her fear drove her out of classes and at times nearly chained her to the house.

All these girls so wanted to be achieving, successful people, yet they were blocked and held back from separating from their families and 'exploring' their worlds. The very symptoms that made them feel such 'helpless babies' demonstrated their fears of being 'adult' and taking the roles that older sisters or brothers had had before. Each of these girls were facing conflict on two fronts. They were struggling with deep fears about separating from home and becoming adults, usually due to highly individual experiences within their own families. They were also facing conflict about becoming successful adults in a world where this is still not easy for girls to be.

## Avoiding the forbidden relationship

Richard, whose therapy was initially sought for him by his wife when he was abroad, was feeling deep despair in his severe conflict. He could see no way of surviving within his marriage and family life with four children, as he felt he was perceived by his wife as 'one of the children'. There had been no sex life between them for a long time and he had been living separately in one of the rooms in the house. He had met a much younger unmarried woman and was contemplating living with her. He oscillated violently between feeling that he also wanted to be with his wife. Yet this was intolerable because he felt like a child in the house and not an equal partner with her, yet he was helpless to alter this. He then moved away from the family towards the new relationship, but that felt equally intolerable because it represented a breakdown of the marriage which he could not bear to let go of.

Richard suffered from acute anxiety whenever he had to make any decision about anything. It was this that had made his wife unable to experience him as a reliable husband. He felt as if *any decision was too difficult to make*, not just the one about leaving home. In his first interview he produced memories of observing his lonely mother when his father was very involved with work. Richard recalled feeling strongly that he could make a 'better husband' for his mother than his father did. This belief was experienced again, when Richard's brother brought his fiancée home. Richard was very critical of his brother's treatment of her, and hugged the same secret thought to himself that he could be a 'better husband' to her than his brother would be. Neither of those wishes could be fulfilled, and both would have brought him into sharp confrontation with his father and brother. As he talked and admitted that these wishes could not be realities, he felt that to let go the *idea* of the wish and to love someone else was a terrible 'betrayal'. He had very great doubts about getting married and felt it only happened because his mother played a big part in persuading him to do so.

When he began therapy he felt that the only woman he could really love was a 'person from the past'. Richard's decision to relate closely to someone now seemed to hold a denial of his love for another, which set up a deep conflict for him. It also seemed that his wishes and desires were for things that he could never have, repeating the pattern of his early longing for his mother. At times he imagined going off and living entirely by himself, but he also knew that would hold intolerable loneliness for him.

Robert, a man in middle age, presented his need for therapy because of a conflict in his life that caused him deep distress. It had not been resolved during a period of psychoanalysis in his early twenties. He felt his 'problem' was getting worse and his feelings of guilt, shame and depression concerning it were increasing. For many years he had felt driven to dress in female clothes – originally his mother's and now his wife's. So dressed, he would ask his wife to tie him up, always in the same way, using belts. This produced enormous levels of sexual arousal and he would then masturbate to orgasm. This 'charade', as it came to be called, had previously been understood with his Freudian psychoanalyst solely in terms of his forbidden sexual desires for his mother and the resulting guilt that he was struggling to overcome. His wife took a very understanding and tolerant view of it and went along with it all. This was done mainly to please him, but also because she felt that she would have to be more involved with him sexually than she wanted, if these needs were thwarted. She and Robert had a 'normal' sex life together which fluctuated between being fairly satisfying to being on occasions very good for them both.

As Robert began to describe the 'charade' in detail, he said how pleased he felt that he was not viewed as a weird or alarming person by the therapist, and that he could feel relaxed and accepted as attention was directed towards understanding his behaviour as a very uncomfortable 'neurotic solution' to a severe state of conflict.

He recalled how at the age of six he had felt so afraid of the world outside that one very stormy day he dressed up in his mother's mackintosh for comfort. He had huge difficulties throughout his childhood in separating from her, and was unable to visit away from home. Much later, following his father's death, he had been completely unable to take up his first really promising job. This was a job he had chosen to do, as distinct from the war service he had been compelled to do and which his mother had accepted.

He remembered setting off to the station and instead of getting on a train to go to his place of work he had gone to a different platform and caught a train going to a place he had never been to before. He was alarmed and confused, and became so panic stricken that he developed such acute pains in the chest that he believed he was having a heart attack. He got on a return train and took himself to an Accident and Emergency Unit of a London hospital. From there, despite a difference of opinion between two doctors, the view that he had a psychological problem won the day and he was referred to a psychoanalyst for therapy. This proved to be helpful and enabled him to take up very suitable work, marry and have a family. The symbolic acting out continued intermittently but became much more compulsive following his mother's death, and increased further when his children left home, giving him greater freedom to carry it out.

The interesting aspect of the 'charade' was that he had to play both parts in the drama, and so he first dressed as his mother and then tied 'her' up (which was the height of the excitement). He was then *both* the helpless tied up 'mother', and the man who had captured her. The moment the act of masturbation was complete he felt that being the tied up woman as well as being the man who had violated her utterly intolerable. His anxiety was then acute until he was freed, which he needed to have done as quickly as possible.

When he was the 'man who had captured her' and was anticipating having her sexually, he could feel very excited and powerful. Once it was over he was in touch with an agonising level of powerlessness – which he saw as the source of his need to 'have her again'. So the 'neurotic solution', although it appeared to give him 'power' over the mother who had seemed all-powerful in his childhood, merely recreated his feelings of powerlessness which drove him to repeat the act. Meanwhile his inability to travel anywhere alone, to walk any great distance from his car, to act fully and freely for himself, remained untouched and not understood. Therefore, his huge sense of guilt about his 'wicked desires', as he perceived them, seemed overwhelming.

## Loss of self

Anthony was torn with conflict about how he could be himself without threatening his father. When we first met he was on sick leave from his job and had been resting at home for some weeks. He not only felt unable to go to work, but at that stage felt unable to venture out of the house. He was sleeping badly, and often felt compelled to get out of bed at night and seek a place to hide in the bedroom. Such feelings were experienced as frighteningly inappropriate to him, as well as to his wife. He spent many hours in his study doing immaculate exercises as the 'pupil', marking them in red ink as the 'teacher'. Anthony had had two previous points of 'breakdown' earlier in his life when he had also felt unable to continue at work. Both had come at stages when promotion was around for him, as it had been on this occasion too. The 'trigger' each time seemed to be when a relationship between a deeply loving father and son were vividly portrayed to him, once on the stage in an opera, and once on television.

Anthony's relationship with his father began dramatically on the day of his birth when, hearing that he had a son, Anthony's father 'collapsed' and took to his bed. Anthony described his father as a very intelligent and ambitious man, but he worked far below his potential ability. He was extremely violent to his wife and sons. When Anthony secured a grammar school place, this again produced a negative response in his father. Struggling to avoid this Anthony became 'sick' with a mysterious, very prolonged and undiagnosed illness that postponed his move to grammar school for many weeks.

For Anthony to develop or to achieve, especially in the sphere of intellectual work, was so threatening to his father that it appeared to Anthony as if it would cause his father to die. Anthony recoiled from the violent physical aspect of his father, rejecting all manual work for himself. Instead he moved to develop his intellectual work exclusively, which actually threatened his father the most. On one occasion Anthony dared to oppose his father by wearing a red shirt, and his father raged at him for 'being like a girl'.

The same stereotype visions of what is 'appropriate' for men can sometimes be experienced *individually*, in just as oppressive and restrictive a manner as they are for women.

These examples of some 'neurotic conflicts' were experienced by the people suffering them as painfully 'inappropriate'. They have been described as they were presented in the early stages of therapy. Some of the experiences of each person have been added to provide a fuller picture of the source of the conflict. Let us now turn to examine the characteristics of these types of conflict to see what they hold in common, while acknowledging that each one has its own unique variations and many complications because of its individual history.

# 4 Recognising the 'Neurotic Solution'

The 'neurotic solution' is generally quite easily recognised because it has such clear characteristics. It is always easier to recognise other people's 'neurotic solutions' than one's own! The first of these characteristics is how *inappropriate* such solutions are felt to be by the person driven to put them into practice. The woman who feels too frightened to go out of her house knows that to stay at home lessens her fears. Sometimes women who have been severely abused by their husbands actually choose to stay at home to avoid the violence or abuse stirred by any attempt to go out and be more independent. On the other hand, to be a prisoner in her own home feels totally inappropriate. She watches her neighbours go off to work or shop and longs to have their normality.

This aspect of 'inappropriateness' has already been described in some detail in the previous chapter. It is raised again in order to emphasise the need to be watchful about oppressive attitudes in society that may bring about seemingly inappropriate behaviour. Professional carers in particular need to keep these attitudes constantly open to question.

## The compulsive nature of 'neurotic solutions'

People who are struggling to find a solution to an unbearable conflict feel driven to behave in certain ways even when they are aware that these ways are not how they really want to be. They are also aware that they have felt, said or done whatever it is, *so many times before*. Yet this behaviour has not resulted in their achieving what they want for themselves.

During therapy people have the opportunity to examine slowly and in detail both when it is, and in what sort of situations, that these behaviours occur. As they look at how frequently they recur, they often express the feeling that at that particular time *no other way of behaving feels known to them*. It seems as if alternatives have been shut out of their mind, however much they dislike the ones that they feel driven to do.

**The characteristic of persistence**

Another characteristic of the 'neurotic solution' is its persistence. For the person experiencing it, it is as if the need to behave in the same old way is never ending and that the conflict is incapable of solution. For people who feel they have to withdraw; push people away who come too close; feel that they must have an alcoholic drink; must not eat; work late into the night; or whatever the compulsive behaviour may be, it is as if no choice exists, because to change their behaviour would bring about unbearable anxiety or distress.

Margaret (see 'Keeping people alive' in Chapter 3) feels she *must* take the book on diets round to her student because she feels so 'bad' if she does not. Christine feels that she *cannot* go into school assembly when she fears publicly wetting herself. For Richard ('Avoiding the forbidden relationship' in Chapter 3), to make a decision that he will get a divorce leaves him shaking with fear as if he was contemplating a total impossibility. The strength of these compulsive forces and their persistence never ceases to amaze me, no matter how many times I hear them described by others or experience them in myself.

The destructive element in these compulsive urges to carry out the 'neurotic solution' can be immense. It not only drives some people to suicidal feelings, but it often leads them to damage themselves. It is common for women who have been incest victims to give themselves the same severe pain that was originally inflicted on them by their fathers. Through these acts they not only demonstrate, but also actually maintain, the belief that they are 'bad' and 'dirty', although this image is always horrendous for them.

Drink and drugs are often used destructively as well. Whenever James faced a perception of himself as a competent adult he felt compelled to push it away by drinking himself into a stupor. James had great doubts about being an adult and accountable in the world, because he was fearful of the 'damage' he might do. The beginning of these fears was when as a child he was told that his 'bad' behaviour had led to his mother's death. Again and again he sought the 'neurotic solution' of being the 'non-accountable child'. Yet he missed all the satisfaction of feeling like an adult in a way that was good and safe for him. He also knew that his compulsive need to drink to blot these feelings out was courting disaster and could ultimately destroy him.

**'Neurotic solutions' created for survival**

The most important characteristic of 'neurotic solutions', and the reason why we put them into practice with such incredible tenacity, is that when they are first chosen *we believe them to be necessary for our survival*. Once we understand that this is how they were originally experienced, it is no wonder that clients in therapy express acute anxiety at even thinking about change, let alone carrying it out. Nobody can remain calm and talk rationally about letting go of ways of behaving that were originally created to protect them from life-threatening situations. It is for this reason that therapists need to work slowly, to appreciate the courage it takes for people to face these deep fears and to talk about them. Such work can only be done in small amounts at one time.

**'The return of the repressed'**

Freud provided an explanation of why we persist in repeating certain patterns of behaviour in his theory of 'The Return of the Repressed'. This is a very complicated theory, but in ordinary language it means that the very method we choose to solve unbearable conflict actually recreates it. The word 'repressed' means that the feelings have been pushed out of our awareness, so that we *do not know about them*. This does not make them go away, and they reappear in a disguised form in the 'neurotic solution'. This is not recognised by the person involved, who is striving to escape from their painful feelings.

As the feelings reappear, albeit in a new form, so more preventative action is required. This means the 'neurotic solution' is put into practice even harder. Hence we see how the compulsive nature and persistence of neurotic solutions are endlessly recreated.

## The characteristic of hopelessness

This recreation of the original fears also explains the sense of hopelessness so characteristic of the neurotic solution. We may all at times feel deeply convinced that such solutions must be carried out to protect us from some deeply threatening fears, but in reality such solutions solve nothing. Most people who put such solutions into practice feel exhausted, trapped and despairing, like a rat caught in a wheel. The more the rat runs the faster he has to keep moving.

## Giving away self as a 'neurotic solution'

Pamela's 'neurotic solution' holds a very obvious 'Return of the Repressed'. She had a deep sense of not being a person of worth as a girl, because she believed her two brothers were the only valued children in her family. Not surprisingly she turned to a man to provide all her good feelings about herself. She felt that she needed a man to leave his wife for her in order to prove her importance. When this did not happen she became desperately afraid, chasing him and striving to get him to love her until every waking hour was given over to the pursuit of his love. In order to keep up this effort everything else had to be rendered valueless in case it distracted her. As he backed off, making false promises and leaving her feeling let down, she became more and more desperate. She cried, feeling she needed him, she offered him sex whenever he wanted it in the hope that he would stay with her. She felt that she might as well be dead if he no longer loved her. She stopped bothering with meals, washing, or going out with friends, as if nothing mattered but her relationship with him. She continually believed that only his love would provide the solution to her happiness. Yet the more she handed over power to him to determine her life the more lost, inadequate and empty she felt. Such total dependency on a man actually confirmed her deepest fear that being a woman was in itself valueless. In turning to a male to provide her self-esteem she was in constant fear that he would leave her, and confirm her worst fear that she was not worth his loving. This recreated the early sense of terror at having no comfortable identity of her own.

When we feel driven to demand that someone *else* provides proof that we are 'all right', the *less all right* we feel. Such a relationship holds a painfully deep imbalance within it, confirming the worthless feelings from which we are trying to escape. This experience is in complete contrast to the sense of increased strength and joy that grows out of an equal relationship, when the sense of identity of each person is increased through a loving bond.

Let us move from this clear individual example to some generalised examples of the 'Return of the Repressed' familiar to everyone.

## The 'bully'

The 'bully' is a name given to describe a certain type of person. Of course, no-one is wholly bully and so it is more realistic to examine bullying behaviour. The person who has a compulsive need to 'bully' seeks out another who is vulnerable and perceived as 'weak', in order for the 'bully' to hurt them. In the process the 'bully', who always deep down feels himself to be unloved, unworthy and above all powerless, hopes to lift himself up from these feelings by the sense of power he has over his victim.

The method or 'solution' of lifting oneself 'up' through putting someone else 'down' is, however, always ultimately self-defeating. This is because people who bully others never do feel *really* good, or worthy, in any fulfilling sense. All they have done is to *give someone else* who is 'easy prey' the experience of being 'hurt', which the bully himself feels deep inside. The feelings have not been got rid of, but merely duplicated.

Sometimes people who behave in this way can, in their more enlightened moments, actually see what they have been doing. When this occurs they generally condemn their own behaviour very harshly. It seems that such people who then turn to the chastising of themselves partly do so because they genuinely despise their own behaviour, but also as a way of protecting themselves from criticism.

If we 'damn' ourselves first, we are less likely to be damned by others! Apology, providing it is sincere, is the best form of defence against retaliation. Unfortunately, because of the way our society is structured the woman is most frequently the more vulnerable person in a heterosexual relationship, particularly if she has children. This makes women particularly prone to bullying from male partners when the compulsive need to hurt dominates the relationship. I believe it is only occasionally that this arises with a female partner who in turn is compulsively seeking to be hurt. Even when this is the case I believe such women also long to escape from this conflict. If they are seeking pain it is only because early patterns have been set up, leaving them with the belief that to endure suffering is their lot in life. This can occur in a woman who has been sexually and physically abused by her parents who then marries a man who continues to abuse her. The last thing such women need is a suggestion that they 'deserve' it. They should never be condemned because they may *appear* to seek it. They need a great deal of sensitive help and support in changing their belief systems about themselves, so that they can be in control of their lives and find better ways of feeling about themselves. This is one of the major tasks of therapy and why the process cannot be hurried.

One of the facts about people who behave in bullying ways is that they are very fearful of those they perceive as powerful above them. This is because they expect in turn to be hurt or 'put down' by others. This has always been the bully's earliest experience. The only 'gain' from bullying is the short-lived excitement that may come at the time of the bullying incident. Afterwards, at a deeper level, the bully always feels worse. He knows that the victim is undeserving of the hurt and also how that pain feels. His guilt feelings, generally operating just below the bully's awareness, actually serve to maintain 'bad' feelings about himself. These are the very ones from which he was trying to escape through the bullying acts in the first place, but sadly they merely perpetuate the cycle of violence.

## The 'deserted' child

Another equally well-known example of the 'Return of the Repressed' comes about in the person who rejects a deeply longed for attachment, or love relationship, because of the fear that they will lose it.

One of the clearest examples of this is when a small child is separated from its mother. Some years ago this was a very common occurrence whenever a little child went into hospital. Small children in hospital feel deserted and uncomprehending of why their mother, whom at this point is particularly needed, has 'gone away'.

When the child's mother comes to visit, particularly if there has been a gap of some days, she finds her child turning away from her. Nowadays separation more commonly occurs because the mother has been in hospital. This is due to an enormous improvement of awareness in hospitals where children are the patients; but it is less usual for young children to visit their ill parents.

The 'turning away' is not because the child has 'forgotten' its mother (a very superficial explanation that was offered at one stage). It is because the child is now rejecting its mother. This is not because the child does not love her, or need her as much as ever, but it is a chosen 'solution' to avoid the pain of being attached and belonging to someone of utmost importance who then 'goes away'. The pain of risking another loss seems too great to bear.

The child's solution is not to trust a close relationship or not to have it. This is because the choice of 'none' is perceived as *less risky* than being very close and giving *someone else the power* to withdraw the love. The paradox that remains inside this 'neurotic solution' and why it is a perfect example of the 'Return of the Repressed' is that *in the very turning away, the child determines that there will be no mother love for him.* Yet this is the very thing that the child has such dread of losing.

I believe that when we choose to reject the thing we most want, because of deep fears about having it, making us vulnerable to the risk of its loss, we choose one of the worst of all 'neurotic solutions'. The sense of gaining control through rejection is a false one. We remove our energies from the task of finding ways of getting what we really want. In the process we cling to the choice of having 'nothing', and experience the greatest sense of loss of control which lies at the heart of all conflict.

In some cases the need to reject, even to the lengths of getting rid of the object or person whose love we deeply need because we fear it will not be available, can lead to the most violent and destructive behaviour. It is this that can cause a rejected lover to attack a previously loved partner.

Sometimes the ways in which we recreate the very feelings that we are trying to avoid experiencing can be very complicated indeed, and extremely difficult to recognise. Once again such ways of behaving are easier to observe in others rather than in oneself. Let us now turn to examine the appearance of the 'Return of the Repressed' in the 'neurotic solutions' of some of the people whose histories we have started to share.

Margaret, (see 'Keeping people alive' in Chapter 3), hated being the 'bad fairy' and believed she was someone who could harm others. She felt she could even be responsible for their death if she did not work hard to keep them alive, so she set herself the life-long task of trying to do this. It soon became painfully obvious to her that one does not need to struggle to keep people alive unless one particularly fears feeling responsible for their death. This activity of 'keeping people alive' actually exposed the belief that she had the power to cause their death. At a more complicated level, Margaret realised that her sense of futility and despair came from the fact that in reality she had set herself a task in which she was bound to fail. She could not stop people from dying, even though she behaved as if she could. She spent so much energy and time trying to do so that the exhaustion and resentment that followed often overwhelmed her. She experienced a sense of helplessness that stemmed from attempting an impossible task. It also prevented her from finding out that she could let this task go and nothing dreadful would happen.

An obvious example of the 'Return of the Repressed' is shown in Jean's 'solution' (in 'No space' in Chapter 3). Her deep fear of having 'no place in life' was actually recreated by her when she turned to drink to provide 'oblivion'. An attempt to 'free herself' from the pain of those thoughts, through alcohol, brought it back as a sharp reality the following day when she was 'too ill' to go to work, or was perceived by her supervisor as incapable of the job she wanted to do.

The way in which Rebecca kept to the fore all that she wanted to hide is a very good example of a quite complicated 'Return of the Repressed'. (See 'Fear of being successful' in Chapter 3.) She tried to deny the existence of her son because he was evidence of her 'achieving', and so risked arousing deep guilt feelings. One might expect that she would then keep a very 'low profile'. Instead, however, Rebecca chose a name for her son which was actually so unusual it kept the existence of the child constantly to the fore. Rebecca achieved this by endlessly thinking, talking and anticipating what a 'stupid' and 'peculiar' name it was, and how it showed up her own 'worthlessness as a mother'. The reality was that no-one was going to be allowed to forget him for a moment!

For Christine, Alice and Jane (see 'Compulsive fear of "being a baby"' in Chapter 3), their hated symptoms of fear of wetting or soiling made travelling extremely difficult, and also brought back the 'Return of the Repressed' in a very tangled way. They all wanted to 'grow up', to move away from their families normally and free of guilt. Yet all produced 'baby' symptoms which in different ways forced their parents to show extra concern for them and a great deal of attention, giving the 'whiphand' to the girls. They controlled their parents quite powerfully. Within the apparent 'helplessness' recognised in practice by their parents, which involved taking their daughters around in cars and, in Jane's case, agreeing to be available every minute of every day in case she needed them, there was a hidden reversal of roles. These girls achieved the parental caring they desired, albeit at a very high price.

Sometimes we recreate the very situation we most fear in quite small ways. For example when Anthony (in 'Loss of self', in Chapter 3), returned to work and felt much more sure of himself, he planned to do a higher degree and set himself the task of learning a foreign language. He found himself a good local teacher and felt optimistic and happy. However, when his first piece of homework was criticised he became extremely distressed.

The 'neurotic solution' that came immediately to mind was to reject the teacher and abandon learning. In other words, he was behaving just like the child in hospital who turned away from his mother. He was choosing 'no Russian' in preference to running the risk of having his Russian 'taken from him' and made unpleasant by his teacher's criticism. The power he was investing in his teacher was immense, as if Anthony believed he could not survive the teacher's criticism. When Anthony recognised he was choosing 'no Russian' in preference to 'imperfect Russian', thus giving himself a far greater loss, he decided that it was a false solution. He learnt that the criticism could actually be perceived as constructive and that he could use it to learn and enjoy his Russian more. He has increased his tolerance of imperfection in himself and the reward for this is an increased knowledge and pleasure in learning the Russian language.

## Mechanisms used to maintain 'neurotic solutions'

The more we examine 'neurotic solutions' the more complex and maze-like we find them to be. For not only do they exist so strongly in themselves, but they are supported by a series of beliefs that we actually create to maintain them.

For example, the anorexic who has to prove that she or he *must* be in control of their body and weight needs to demonstrate how important this control really is. This can only be done if they engage in behaviour that also demonstrates how easily they can be out of control. This then reinforces the need to keep control. One of the ways of doing this is to develop a belief that they have to finish up all the food, to literally eat everything on the table or in the cupboard. Then they can believe that the only thing that stops an enormous appetite is control from 'outside'. There is literally no food left to eat. Having done this they feel secretly horrified at their own devouring greed, and this reaffirms that the next day, at all costs, such an appetite must be curtailed and they will eat nothing. They really have the 'proof' now to make the control essential.

To give another example, an elderly lady who was still mourning her husband very deeply some years after his death found it impossible to believe that she could manage without him. He had always made all the decisions, and looked after all financial arrangements. When he died she felt increasingly helpless, as if her only solution lay in getting other people to look after her. As she was in reality a competent person, so her inability to take over doing things for herself increasingly distressed her family. She felt more and more isolated from them and became convinced that she could make nothing good happen for herself.

She felt fearful all alone in her large house, and eventually her family found the strain of travelling long distances to help her with her garden too much for them to sustain. A flat became available near to her son's home. Her resistance to this was first shown in her belief that she would 'not live long enough' to move. This was followed by a belief that if she went to live nearby he would be bound to move. Her difficulty in believing that she could organise anything good for herself was immense. Unfortunately, she greeted visitors with the opening remark of 'I bet you wish you'd never come'. This revealed a deep fear of the rejection that she always expected. The very expression she used helped to create people's withdrawal from her, which in turn gave her such sadness.

Some people devote a great deal of energy to maintaining their 'neurotic solutions'. An example of this was shown by a man in his early thirties. He once described his feelings about losing everything that he tried to have when he told the story of his buying some shoes. He was an only child of rather elderly parents, and he had always felt that every achievement had to be denied. He moved from job to job, from relationship to relationship, always intolerant of anything that seemed to be 'succeeding' because he would then have to own or accept responsibility for achieving, which he could not bear to do. He told me how he saw a pair of shoes in a shop window. He needed some and he liked the look of them, but he felt positive they would not be his size. It took him some days to dare to go and find out. Eventually he did, and they were not only his size but they fitted him perfectly. He tried them on, and walked about in the shop. They were right in every way. He could not bring himself to buy them, however, and he continued to regularly look at them in the shop window. He considered them 'his shoes', but he was then in a great state of agitation because now he knew they were perfect and if he did not buy them someone else might do so. Finally he went and bought them. When I asked if he felt happy when he had them, and if he enjoyed wearing them, he shook his head. 'No', he said, 'they are still in a box in my wardrobe. You see, I can't bring myself to wear them, for then they would start to get worn.' They would become less than perfect. His wanting them, his use of them would lead to their destruction.

This story shows so clearly how the beliefs formed in early childhood concerning the 'damage' some people feel their very existence will bring about, can last right on into adulthood, and render them incapable of ordinary acts such as buying clothes for themselves.

### 'Tell me you love me'

One of the simple and commonly met 'neurotic solutions' that provides a 'Return of the Repressed' is when someone feels so anxious and insecure about being loved that they ask their partner to *tell* them that they love them. Very often a partner will respond to this by saying rather unconvincingly that 'I do love you'. It rarely satisfies the person who has asked, for more than a very short time. The very fact that the loving statement comes *only* in response to a request makes it feel of little real value. If instead the person is able to express openly that they feel unsure of their partner's love, and the reasons for this, then some more promising communication may develop between them.

### What do we hear, when we listen?

It seems that we all engage in remarkably complicated mechanisms to shore up our belief systems. But this is no wonder considering we originally created them as necessary for our very survival. John Bowlby (1930) suggests that the way we all *process* information acts as the best protection we have, for not 'knowing' the things we do not want to know. He suggests that we are able to 'filter', to 'keep out' ideas that challenge our ways of thinking. I believe this is a very important contribution to our understanding. It is not a new idea in itself, for have we not the old sayings, 'There's none so deaf as those who do not want to hear; nor blind, as those who do not wish to see.' What is interesting, however, is that we can actually hold, at a clear level of awareness, two totally contradictory pieces of information. We shut one out, and behave as if the other is the only true version, as a method of avoiding the conflict and the need to solve it that would otherwise occur.

An example of this is the person quoted in Chapter 2 who always felt so 'hurt' if someone else displayed knowledge that she did not have, and spoke of the pain that came from realising that she 'did not know'. Simultaneously she asked 'What is wrong with not knowing?' This seemed to suggest that she knew there was nothing 'wrong' with it; yet that knowledge did not resolve or even lessen her feelings of pain. Perhaps she was really asking herself the question of why could she not believe that. Why could she not feel that it was safe not to have knowledge of certain things and that she need not feel 'put down' by other's knowledge?

Many people experience other people's knowledge and achievements as if they were their own loss. This is because other's knowledge or their position has been experienced in the past as being a source of power that was intimidating. For many adults who frequently experience this sense of loss, there is nearly always a history of this having occurred for them in painful ways in their early life. I would support Alice Miller's (1983) view that such adults have had insufficient parental care and love. A very dominant parent may have deprived them of good feelings about themselves. Such children can become highly competitive as they compulsively continue their search for parental love and approval. Alice Miller points out that most frequently any clear memory concerning feelings about these experiences is actually denied. The childhood experiences are exposed again and again by the adult behaving in exactly the same way as he or she was treated in their own childhood.

It seems that this 'shutting of our minds', this virtual *inability to hear* what might provoke too deep a challenge to our belief systems, may well be the most effective method that we use to prevent us from changing. This seems to be so, regardless of the pain and distress that may be present, because we so deeply fear exposing ourselves to any need for change.

## The trigger event

There is one more characteristic of the 'neurotic solution' that is important to recognise. It is that the conflict which demands a solution can be seen in quite minor occurrences as well as in those major ones that can sometimes last many years.

When people first seek therapy, one of the most valuable ways of understanding the nature of their problem is to listen very carefully to their view about whatever incident or particular feeling they consider made them seek therapy at this particular time. This can often be seen as a *current version* of the way they struggle to put the 'neurotic solution' into practice.

Often the conflicts that they describe will have been going on for a very long time. When attention is focused on the immediate present, however, there is nearly always a keen awareness that something of importance has either just happened or is about to happen. This is the 'trigger' event. I believe that when these events are examined with care they help us to understand the nature of the conflict as well as the attempted solutions. This is because the 'trigger' event always holds either a new form of the original conflict, or is a repeat, yet again, of the old form of it. It is often experienced by the person as the proverbial 'straw that broke the camel's back'. Because it is so immediate it can be recognised more easily as yet another example of the person struggling to put the old 'neurotic solution' into practice and finding it impossibly difficult to do so.

For Margaret (in 'Keeping people alive' in Chapter 3), it was in her neighbour's sudden and huge increase in demand for support, because of the death of her husband. This created for Margaret a 'replay' of the situation in her own life as a child, and also highlighted her conflict. She felt compelled to give a great deal of care to this neighbour, and yet she resented giving it and feared being swamped and exhausted. For Rosemary (Chapter 3) it was her boyfriend's offer of marriage almost simultaneously as his discussion of his obsessive love for another that triggered her request for therapy.

For Jean ('No space', Chapter 3), the 'trigger' was the perilous point of the examination 're-sit'. She was uncertain whether she could obtain a 'place' in her newly-chosen career and that it was most likely she would fail again, once more experiencing the terrifying sensation of 'no space for her' that she believed was her 'lot in life'.

For Anthony (see 'Loss of self' in Chapter 3), the 'trigger' was yet another offer of promotion, bringing with it the possibility of his own progress, coupled with the old feeling that he must not take it because of the dire consequences he always associated with the collapse of his father if Anthony moved to 'better' himself. It was actually seeing a visual presentation of a loving father and son that reminded Anthony of his deep sense of loss, of having a father who was violent and rejected him.

The 'trigger' event is not only an example of an event which always holds *the same ingredients as the basic conflict*, but it also exposes to the person the fundamental hopelessness of the 'neurotic solution'. Margaret cannot be 'husband' to her neighbour nor can she 'repair the damage' of his death. Rosemary's love, however consistent, does not prevent her partner's betrayal. Jean solves nothing by drinking and becoming incapable of sitting her examination. Anthony cannot live happily as he is constantly denying his abilities.

# 5 Working Through: Bringing about Change

## What is 'mental pain'?

People talk of having 'bad nerves' or 'breaking down' or fearing that they are 'going mad'. These phrases mean different things to different people, but common to them all is the experience of severe 'mental pain'. It is hard to separate 'mental pain' from 'bodily pain', because mental anguish consists of *painful feelings* which always produce unpleasant sensations in our bodies.

When anyone is in a severe state of conflict, certain feelings are experienced very strongly. The most usual one is anxiety. If this is severe it produces bodily sensations which are overwhelming and feel utterly intolerable. Conflict which feels unresolvable can also produce deep depression. Bouts of uncontrollable crying are the commonest bodily expression of these feelings, but for others a sense of inertia occurs, springing from a belief that nothing is worth doing. Someone in this state can feel unable to move, uninterested in eating and so detached from themselves that they feel numb and totally disinterested in anything. At such a time the person feels hardly able to give any value to themselves.

Less severe feelings of depression leave some people feeling that their need for care will be experienced as so vast that it can never be met. They fear that their great need will drive others away. This confirms to the depressed person that their 'greediness' is unacceptable and that they are 'unworthy' of care. Although they feel that they are without any energy to care for themselves, they sometimes strongly reject care when it is offered, as it merely confirms and increases their own hated sense of helplessness unless this care is offered very sensitively.

Anger is another painful mental state frequently experienced in our bodies. It often comes as a protection against fear which the

48

person does not want to recognise, because they feel they could be overwhelmed by a sense of weakness. Sometimes anger can be a valuable positive feeling if it drives away inappropriate fears, and leads the person out of an oppressed situation. Unfortunately though, expressions of anger often merely reproduce the rejection by others that the angry person was experiencing himself just before the rage came bursting through. Excessive guilt, which is one of the most unpleasant of all mental pains, also has a marked physical aspect to it. This may be because it carries the greatest *mix* of feelings. A deep sense of unworthiness drives us to deeds which often fail to hide the resentment and anger we are also feeling. This can create a sense of confusion and also sometimes one of inexplicable dread. Severe guilt holds so much conflict that it is nearly always experienced bodily in the form of a chronic sense of exhaustion. It can also produce restlessness and acute irritability.

All these feelings vary in strength both between individuals and from time to time within the same person. Some people with severe conflicts only experience one main form of mental pain. Others can experience varieties of all of them. If one feels very anxious it is hard not to feel depressed by it as well. If the depression is an engulfing one it also leads to anxiety. Anger and guilt in severe form always carry other feelings with them. When any of these severe forms of mental pain occur, the one characteristic that they have in common, for the person concerned, is a feeling of being *unable to alter them.* The deepest fear is that the feelings will get out of control. This is what most people mean when they speak of 'breaking down', or fear that they are 'going mad'.

As soon as we start to talk in greater detail of how these feelings of fear, depression, anger or guilt are experienced, we talk of how our bodies behave. We have pain in the 'gut' or the head. Our shoulders or neck ache; we sweat or tremble; tears well up quickly and unexpectedly; we feel dizzy or nauseous; our legs can feel too weak to carry us. All these sensations occur as a result of complicated mechanisms in our bodies. These bodily sensations occur because strong feelings, such as severe depression or acute anxiety, produce certain chemicals in the body. These in turn produce other effects in our bodies which tend to make the feelings even stronger. Anyone who has suffered from blushing or stammering knows this 'spiralling effect' only too well. As the person feels shy or embarrassed, so their face and neck start to flush. As the person feels the blush showing and realises that their fears can no longer be hidden, so the blushing get worse. It is this 'spiralling effect' that can lead to panic and the dreaded sensation of loss of control.

A young man gave a good example of this, as he described what happened when he was asked to speak at a wedding. He felt very worried that he might stammer or blush, that his mouth would dry up and that he would be unable to speak at all. In the event these symptoms did begin to appear, and as he realised his fears were being exposed to the guests so he began to feel worse. It was only by a tremendous effort and a realisation that his audience was not such a critical one that he managed to complete his speech. The method he used to overcome the fear was effective, because he was able to get a clue about the source of his fear and then to provide reassurance for himself.

When we examine long-term mental pain, we see that it arises from conflicts that are deeply embedded in people's way of life. There seem to be two quite distinct *sources* of mental pain. The kind of pain that is experienced feels different according to its source. Let us move to examine these and to understand ways of recognising why the source of the pain plays such an important part in determining our feelings.

**Two sources of mental pain**

The first kind of pain is to do with struggling to *face* the situation or attain the *wished for object* which, though longed for, often feels 'too difficult' to reach or to hold on to. This is because the goal the person now seeks *originally held such terror*. The form that it took in childhood was experienced as unbearable, so that this mental pain or distress always feels to the person concerned the hardest thing to cope with. It often feels quite impossible! Jim struggles with it as he walks to the door of the firm where he has to face a buyer. Jean confronts it when she goes to work deeply fearing another 'slap down' from her superiors. Margaret battles with it as she feels she will not be good enough for her evening class students. For Jennifer it comes whenever she wants anything for herself. Jane faces it as she starts to get on the bus. For Anthony even to open his Russian textbook and to start reading it produces a feeling of anguish, because of what he fears he will have to 'pay' for any enjoyment.

For many people suffering from deep, life-long conflict, these feelings of fear and dread arise simply as they move towards making contact with others in quite ordinary situations. This is because they are expecting to feel the same fearful sensations of being unloved, rejected, or in some sense 'bad' or 'at fault' that they originally experienced. For many women it is quite common to be treated as unimportant or to feel under-valued. Their deep fear is that they will never be able to make themselves heard, or have their feelings valued. For all these people the *wish* to do these things is there, but the fear that arises as they attempt to do so is overwhelming.

The second kind of mental pain comes as a *result of putting the 'neurotic solution' into practice*, and of not making any headway with the original wish. It is nearly always accompanied by feelings of depression, frustration, defeat, and for some a sense of self-hatred. It feels to the person like 'giving in' or 'giving up', and that the wish to do whatever it was felt 'too difficult'. It often leaves a deep sense of guilt, especially when this involves broken promises within a close relationship. It can take many other forms too. For example, Lorna, a woman with teenage children, longed to travel about freely but felt unable even to cross the road. She described deep feelings of regret and guilt that her children missed out on holidays abroad and visits to interesting places because she felt unable to take them.

When Jim's sense of his 'tiny penis' and his shaking anxiety made him drive past the firm he planned to call on, he said to himself: 'I'll go tomorrow.' He is no longer fighting the first type of pain, and he gets an immediate sense of relief. But the second type of pain begins to form and the feelings of failure and a generalised sense of depression appear instead.

Jean has gone out to buy herself a bottle of some alcoholic drink, thereby confirming her feelings that she is not strong enough to face her superior's criticism. She is ready to believe she will never be appreciated and the very need for the bottle feels like an agreement with this dismal view of herself. This is followed by her feeling sick or being unable to take any action at all to better or improve her situation.

Margaret decides to give up her classes and relieve herself from the fear that she may fail her students in some way. She is left, however, with great unease.

Jennifer goes out alone instead of visiting a friend. She convinces herself that she is missing nothing as the friend will only talk about her problems and will not listen to Jennifer's. In this way she tries to rationalise away the value of friends and strengthen the belief that she is safer without one, but her loneliness is painful.

As Anthony cannot manage to open his Russian books, he spends all evening looking at the outside of them and loses an evening he might have spent studying with enjoyment. Robert cannot go to the shop, which he feels is too far away from the car park and returns home without a purchase that he wants. Almost immediately a headache sets in and sometimes a sense of acute depression.

The first cause of mental pain is to do with struggling with the fears involved in *trying to achieve something*. The second is to do with the feelings that come *because the fears have prevented it being achieved*. When the source is of the second kind the pain always includes a great deal of explaining, excusing and a 'bolstering up' of the belief that the 'wish' (now given up) was either not really wanted, or would have been of no real use. This is the well-known 'sour grapes' mechanism that we use to save ourselves from bearing with the pain of wanting what we cannot have. Instead we turn it, in our minds, into something not worth having. At this point, the original 'old belief' has taken over; the 'neurotic solution' has been put into practice yet again. The agoraphobic cannot go out, and the dismal hopeless feelings dominate again.

As Jane goes once more in the parental car, because she could not face the bus with no access to a toilet, so she increases her belief that the bus is not a possible way for her to travel. Whenever this choice is made, it tends to confirm the belief that putting the desired goal into practice is 'impossible'.

### Using an understanding of the past to help with the present

In order to break through these 'it's impossible to do' feelings and to start making a change, it is necessary for the person to make *sense* of why they feel as they do. Though such feelings often make no 'sense' in the current situation, it is helpful to recognise that *at an earlier time they did so*. They were built up at a time when certain early perceptions of a situation were formed. As time has gone by these perceptions have become increasingly inappropriate, but the *response* in similar situations has not changed.

### Feeling like the 'wrong person'

Let us listen to Marjorie's story. She was the second of two girls. The first-born child had been a boy who only survived a few months. The second pregnancy was an attempt to replace the lost son, but it 'failed' as the child was a girl. The parents decided to try again and another girl was born. At this point the parents gave up on producing a son.

Marjorie's earliest recollections were of 'not being the right person', although she tried very hard to play the boyish games that pleased her father. Marjorie felt that she never fitted in, that she was the 'stupid' one who was forever compared unfavourably with her brilliant elder sister.

Marjorie's solution to this unbearable situation of being unable to be the 'wanted son' was to hide. She felt she must not show herself, or even *be* herself, for that was to experience herself as the 'wrong person'. She strove all the time to be the person *other people said she should be*.

When she first started to talk about her feelings, she cried with a deep sense of loss. Her tears were for all the years she felt that she had lost being 'unable to be herself'. Whenever Marjorie made a move to make a relationship or a home, she withdrew or felt unable to fully carry it out. At times she felt that she did not know who she was. This was because she had so habitually crushed her own wishes that they were barely known to her. As Marjorie slowly began to recognise *why* she had chosen to 'hide' as a 'solution', she also saw how the hiding was in itself a source of

severe distress. It was a 'neurotic solution' and totally inappropriate
in denying her real needs, and she saw how it had led her to feel
many times like an observer rather than a full participator in life.

## Understanding the two 'sides' of conflict

Therapy provides us with the opportunity to recognise the two
'sides' of our conflicts, and most important of all how to understand
the connection between the two.

As people begin to talk about aspects of their life that they feel
are unbearable it is often possible to discover quite quickly what
it is that they are feeling that they must do or not do, in spite of
hating it or experiencing deep distress about it.

It takes longer to hear about the early experiences that provided
them with certain beliefs about themselves. For example, for
Margaret (see pages 18–21) that her desires for something for
herself led to her father's death. For Rosemary (see pages 21–2)
that her very existence prevented her mother escaping from her
marriage. For Anthony (see pages 31–2) that any progress of his,
damaged his father. Such beliefs are so intolerable that they
demand a solution, and these have to be formulated at a time
when the child knows very little, but feels very intensely. The
solution is sought as a 'survival technique' and it sets the pattern
the person continues to engage in from then on, with the compulsive
repetitive persistence described in the previous chapter.

As therapy continues the person slowly recognises why they set
up the compulsive need to put the 'neurotic solution' into practice.
Simultaneously they begin to see why its inappropriateness
increases. It is this current inappropriateness that is now facing
them with unbearable conflict, because the 'neurotic solution'
which they feel compelled to put into practice is giving them as
much pain as did the original belief. Once this stage is reached,
nearly all the remaining therapy time is given to supporting and
encouraging the client as they try to behave differently. They
slowly and painfully work to discover that what they wish to do
may be possible after all. It does not always have to be 'solved' or
'sabotaged' by the compulsive 'neurotic solution'. Margaret does
not have to keep everyone alive; Marjorie does not have to hide
and Jean can make her own safe 'space'.

As they work through these experiences they all become able to see the two 'sides' of the conflict. 'A' is the longed for position and 'Z' the neurotic solution which prevents 'A' occurring. Soon the discovery is made that because 'A' was originally felt to be 'dangerous', it continues to bring 'Z' up in strong opposition to prevent 'A' occurring *as if the person's survival was still at risk*.

Marjorie (feeling the 'wrong person', see page 53) realises that she has to try and seek 'A' (coming out of hiding) in spite of the fear. She has to recognise and challenge her 'Z' position (the feeling that she must hide). She starts to question whether it is really necessary to hide every time she feels that she 'has to'. She starts to risk 'being seen', saying what she thinks, choosing how she wants things done, and in the process she discovers that at last she is not doomed always to be the 'wrong person'.

Let us examine how the wish for 'A' has led to the 'Z' position for other people whose stories we are sharing.

Margaret wanted loving and close relations, *free* of the fear that this very 'wanting' could kill the person she loved (her 'A' position). In direct conflict with this was her belief that she *could cause* the people she loved to die, and she must therefore work hard to keep them alive. This was her compulsive 'Z' position. But this 'neurotic solution', to work hard to keep them alive, produced great resentment and exhaustion, and became an unbearable position to maintain.

As Margaret began to look at how her 'A' position related to the 'Z' one, she began to dare to experiment. She realised that it was because of her father's death that she *believed* that she could cause those she loved to die. Once she saw where this belief belonged, but *that it was not an absolute truth for all time*, so she could let it go – and with it the compulsive need to work to keep others alive.

Margaret began to do just 'enough' for people, and tried to limit this so that she never did anything she would resent. She began to find the courage to say 'no' and to discover that nothing terrible happened. Instead, she began to feel freer, more energetic, and she began to see the way out of her burdensome conflict.

When Jean (see page 22) allowed herself to risk making a close relationship with an old friend who valued her greatly, she experienced the reality of some 'space' being there for her. In discovering it *was* there, that she *could* feel wanted, she could believe that she might actually seek it in other places as well.

Jennifer slowly realised that it was the intense fear that her artwork would be rejected and that she would not get the approval she sought so compulsively that actually prevented her painting in a creative way. It sometimes led her to destroy her pictures or feel less and less satisfied with the outcome of her painting. She began to cut herself off from nearly all other commitments or distractions in order to concentrate on painting even more intensely, because she badly wanted their acceptance and to be valued through them. This was her 'A' position but she very successfully sabotaged it, sometimes in a very openly destructive way (her 'Z' position).

Sometimes the swing from the 'A' to 'Z' can be bizarre and alarmingly paradoxical for the person experiencing it. For example, the person who may relate lovingly to someone one day can also turn them into someone they have to reject the next, when loving feels too frightening to bear. This occurs in people who believe that to be 'loved' is to be 'taken over', with a risk of rejection that feels too great for them to bear.

## The 'back to square one' feeling

For many people the 'Z' position, when it suddenly reappears, is experienced as being 'back to square one'. At first, when something of 'A' is achieved, it almost inevitably produces a swing to 'Z'. This, then, tends to feel more entrenched than ever, and the struggle can feel 'too great'. This is the time when the therapist needs to offer the strongest support and understanding and to share all the experience available to convince the client that such feelings are to be expected.

As the person strives towards 'A' and then experiences the reappearance of 'Z', they have to recognise for themselves that 'Z' has reappeared *because* 'A', though wanted, carries fear embedded within it. 'Z' has been created by them as a 'solution' to the fear, but of course it deprives the person of 'A' which they so deeply wish for. This 'working through' process consists of *many* swings from 'A' to 'Z' until gradually each person discovers 'A' can be had, sufficiently free of fear, and that 'Z' is a useless 'solution' because it brings depression and despair.

This connection between the two sides of the conflict slowly becomes apparent. If Jane manages to get on the bus on Monday – in other words she achieves the 'A' position – then on Tuesday she will probably not even be able to get to the bus stop. This is because the 'Z' position has had to work more strongly than ever to reassert itself in response to 'A' being so 'successful'.

Therapists who describe themselves as 'behaviourists' have shown that certain specific fears, such as travelling in a lift or being in a room with a feared animal, can sometimes be 'broken' through if the person can be helped to experience and tolerate their fear without huge anxiety. However, when fears are deep rooted, long lasting and embedded in ways of living, there is no simple or smooth progression out of them. The fact is, the more and the harder people work towards their 'A' position, the *greater* the 'Z' position recurs in opposition.

Psychoanalysts call this 'working with resistance'. It actually means that the beliefs Jane has held that have driven her to solve her conflict about leaving home, by feeling unable to get on the bus, have been deeply challenged when she achieves it. She has been on the bus, proving that she *can* go on it. This fact conflicts with the belief that such a level of freedom in travelling is 'dangerous'. This leads Jane to resist the change more firmly than ever; despite her longing to get on the bus again the compulsive neurotic solution is now reasserted to prevent any further progress.

### Not 'relapse' but 'backlash'

Once people understand, by observing their own behaviour, that 'A' actually tends to create 'Z' they stop talking, as psychiatrists tend to do, in terms of 'relapse'. This sounds as if the person has returned to some hopeless state again, never to recover. Instead, careful observation enables the person to see that a 'backlash' has occurred. This is, I believe, both a more correct perception and a far more hopeful one. It should be available as part of real understanding for all people in a state of severe conflict.

Making the effort to change the old pattern, to strive towards one's wish, inevitably brings the 'sabotage' of the old neurotic solution. This needs to be recognised as a 'backlash', talked about and if possible examined, not with despair, but with interest!

People can learn as much from the pain they experience from 'backlash' – that is the re-emergence of the 'Z' position – as they can from breaking through to 'A'. When did it happen? Why? Did they try to do too much 'A' too fast? Quite often even a statement that they feel happy, or that they have achieved something they wanted to do, brings up the 'sabotage' and the sense of achievement has to be spoilt.

The importance of this observation is that it gives the person involved an opportunity to see just how 'dangerous', at some level of thinking, they still perceive their 'wish' to be. For the 'backlash' shows that 'part' of them will not allow themselves to have it! They still hold within themselves opposition to it, and they will still try to prevent it occurring. This struggle can go on for a long time for some people.

The encouraging aspect comes when they realise that the severity of the 'backlash' is *exactly equal to the success* of the 'breakthrough'. This recognition can make people almost welcome the backlash, for it is a sign that their 'old beliefs' are really being challenged. At times of course it is not possible to welcome the return of the old painful 'Z' position, but seeing that it has come because of change makes it more bearable. As 'A' is striven for, the 'old beliefs' are 'fighting back' and trying to reassert themselves, but backlash (that means 'Z' following 'A') shows that changes are really beginning. This has to be recognised as not a time to give up therapy, which of course is what the 'backlash' is attempting to make the person believe they should do. Instead, it is a time for increased observation, and to examine yet again the falseness of the 'neurotic solution', how it came about and to see how inappropriate it is.

Jim does not have to have his 'tiny penis' and his fear of buyers. It is not really dangerous for Jane to go on the bus. These are reactions to do with very old fears that no longer apply.

## The importance of small steps

Once someone really understands from their own experience that 'A' brings 'Z' and the reasons for this, then attention is given to how 'A' can be achieved without arousing the 'Z' backlash too much.

The answer always lies in trying to achieve 'A' in small amounts, and experimenting in particular areas or situations that produce less anxiety. Often, for example, 'breakthroughs' (that is, achieving 'A' without the compulsive 'Z' being aroused) come first in areas of work rather than with relationships.

George, for example, knew he wanted to achieve and to succeed in life, yet he realised that in many areas he did not even try. He did not try to write or to speak in public for fear of being criticised. He played chess but frequently lost, though he knew he was a very good player.

As he talked he began to see that he lost games because he made very simple, obvious mistakes due to inattention. He soon realised that he was 'sabotaging' himself. Chess became the first area of his life where he allowed himself to win. Later, he used the understanding he had gained about himself as a chess player to discover that he did not, after all, have to be a 'loser'. He realised that he had actually feared being a 'winner' all his life, for very understandable reasons, and though he had previously thought that that was what he wanted, as he began to examine his own behaviour he saw clearly that he prevented himself having the successful position of being 'winner' because of the anxiety associated with that position.

It is often a great relief to people in therapy to realise that no-one is going to change completely and that no-one needs to do so, in order to free themselves from the worst forms of conflict. What ordinary everyday life provides for us, however, is hundreds of opportunities to behave *differently*. Once people begin to risk trying out something they previously feared, they discover the worst does not inevitably happen. By trying it out in a small way, one is not risking losing all!

Jean (page 22) does not have to strive to secure an entire place for herself in life overnight. If, however, she can risk trying to arrange an outing with a local group or going with a friend to a concert, perhaps neither will come off. However, unless she tries they will never become realities. As she learns that she can survive a small rebuff, and recognises that this is all that it is, so she gradually stops responding as if every rebuff means there is 'no space' for her at all anywhere.

In every 'small example' all the ingredients of the 'A' position exist, and they hold the challenge that leads to the creation of 'Z'.

They are like 'miniatures', representing the basic conflict in some small area. If the person can work through them, knowing that the 'old feelings' will come up but that those can be tested, observed and understood on a small scale, they can often be recognised, borne with and gradually overcome. Slowly, the 'neurotic solution' loses its compulsive force.

Jane discovers that she can get on the bus, even if only for one stop; or she may make her journey differently by bike.

It is important for everyone trapped in conflict to try and do *something*, however small, towards putting the 'wish' into practice. Even if the 'other side' (the 'Z' aspect of the conflict) is still operating most of the time, if some small changes can be made towards 'A' it gives the person experience of discovering that it can be done. Moreover, it is one certain way of preventing mental pain arising from the second source in a severe form.

## Early patterns of feeling

Sometimes, even when people know that their early experiences have led to certain patterns of feeling, they ask with a sense of bewilderment: 'Why do I go *on* feeling them now?' Perhaps nobody yet fully knows why early patterning holds so much strength in determining life-long behaviour in certain people rather than others. It seems probable, however, that three factors play a part. The first is to do with the severity of the fear when the pattern originated. The second concerns whether the same type of situation was experienced again in later childhood or adolescence. The third factor is how far other people or events in the person's life helped to make up for, or counteract, the original experiences.

I would like to take an extreme example first. Graham, a very able man, could never ask for anything for himself, either at home or at work. This was because he felt so fearful of rejection. When he was two years old his mother had put him into the residential care of a sixteen-year-old girl, who lived with her mother and grandmother in a neighbouring village. Some years later, when he returned to his own home, his father returned from the war. Shortly after this his parents' marriage split up. He was taken by his mother at the age of seven to a boarding school, where he was left once again. This time the Headmaster found him alone, sitting on his trunk at the school entrance.

Two deeply traumatic experiences of being abandoned by his mother left Graham needing to find a 'solution' to avoid being exposed to rejection ever again. He was never to ask for anything, and as far as possible never to have anything, for then he would be protected from loss.

He requested therapy as an adult, when he developed a symptom of a phobic fear of cancer. This symptom was removed successfully by a 'short-term', 'behaviourist' type of therapy. However, it was swiftly followed by a more vague, but stronger, fear that he would never live to survive tomorrow. At that point he requested a different type of therapy. As he began to observe himself he saw the link between the severity of his feelings about being abandoned, and his beliefs that he must reject everything, including his enjoyment of every day. Far from enjoying his life each day was something of a private agony to him, as he believed it would be his last.

## Challenging the patterning

However strong the patterning of beliefs may be for any of us, the method of changing them must come *through challenging them*. Everyone who examines their fears with honesty, realises that the beliefs they hold concerning their fears exist in order to prevent themselves achieving something that they want.

So long as Jane (page 10) believes that being on the bus is terrifying, so she will not get on it. By not doing whatever it may be, she is actually being prevented from discovering that it *can* be safe to do it. By experimenting in very small ways, or in limited areas, the person discovers it is possible not to 'listen' to the old fears or ideas that can come to mind. They can begin to see them for what they are, and slowly start to push them away.

James wanted to take up drawing again after a very long break. He bought an easel, pencils and all that he needed, but he could not begin. He so feared failing that he convinced himself that it was better not to draw at all rather than to do a 'poor' picture and experience a sense of disappointment in his own abilities. By not risking 'failing' he actually prevented himself from experiencing

'success'. It was this possibility that he was not allowing himself
to have.

### Recognising 'before', 'during' and 'after'

One of the most helpful observations people can make concerns
*when* they 'sabotage' their own wishes.

For example, Jane's main 'sabotaging' (or 'resistance' as some
therapists prefer to call it) was produced in order to *prevent* her
from getting on the bus. This was to stop her experiencing the
fear associated with ideas around abandoning her family. Jane
does not even attempt to do it, so for her the 'sabotage' occurs
*before* the event. This operates so strongly that she does not get
on the bus.

Jim may telephone a buyer first, fix an appointment and go into
the firm. He has overcome the fears in the 'before' period.
However, if the buyer is large and seems aggressive or sarcastic,
Jim starts to lose his confidence, which he had held onto quite
strongly a few minutes previously in the car park. His hands start
to tremble, his voice goes squeaky and the old anxiety and 'tiny
penis' feelings come on again. This is an example of 'sabotage'
coming on *during* an encounter, in which Jim is trying to put 'A'
into action.

Often, if someone manages not only to push the 'sabotaging'
away and decides to do what they want, and to carry it through
successfully, they expect to feel pleased, relieved and happy about
it. In reality, however, if what they want to do holds very severe
conflict for them, it is not always possible for them to have these
good feelings afterwards. They have succeeded to the 'A' position
and triumphed, but now there is only the period of 'afterwards'
left for the 'sabotage' or resistance to operate in. This nearly
always takes the form of making the person feel completely unable
to repeat or continue with whatever they have achieved, until they
have worked through it many times.

Michael (the man who bought the shoes but could not wear
them) provides a good example of this. He spoke of how much he
wanted to play badminton. He said he was afraid to do so, for
fear he would have a heart attack (an example of sabotage
'before'). After some discussion he decided to go to the doctor

and have his heart examined. He was told that his heart was normal and his doctor encouraged him to play. Michael then described how he had met a friend, booked a court and had an enjoyable game. Afterwards, however, as he sat in the changing room, he became aware that he had sweated a lot during the game. He decided that that was so 'bad' for him that he must be sure he never played again.

This is an example of 'sabotage' reappearing more strongly than ever. It showed Michael that his inability to allow himself to have pleasure was so extreme that having accomplished it (so that by that stage he could not actually prevent it) he was only left with the period of 'afterwards'. In this period he felt compelled to produce new evidence, to make sure that his enjoyment was spoilt and would not lead him to play any further games.

### The same 'intelligence' available to both sides of the conflict

Because Michael's belief that it was 'risky' to enjoy things had been challenged by his playing, he had then felt compelled to produce a new reason to prevent that occurring again. He was able to see, however, that his 'intelligence' worked first on 'one side' of the conflict and then on the other. The part that tried to prevent him having enjoyment could equally well be 'spotted' and challenged, as the part that pressed on to allow himself to play could be recognised too.

Sometimes people can get a sense of relief as they begin to recognise that the same 'intelligence' is as available to the part of them that wishes to do something as it is to the part that tries to resist or 'sabotage' it. It becomes a great challenge to recognise the 'sabotage' and to keep one step ahead of it! Often, to start with, people can only recognise sabotage *after* it has occurred. Later, it can be recognised as it is happening *during* an encounter or event. One of the best ways of doing this is to try and explain what one is feeling to the people one is with, as openly as possible. Sometimes the behaviour or response can then be changed. Eventually, sabotage can be 'spotted' *in advance*, and actually prevented. When this occurs the person really feels in control, and free of the fears that they had because the 'worst has not happened'. They have managed to challenge the long-held beliefs and found them to be no longer true. The person experiences a belief that they can behave and feel as they want to. This may not always be so complete or on every occasion, but they can dare to move towards it, no longer having to deny it or run away from it.

## The experience of change

For most people the first major change occurs as they learn how to lessen the 'Z' position. The 'neurotic solution' is held less compulsively. Gradually it is seen to *belong to the past*, and its inappropriateness to the current situation is felt more keenly. Sometimes at this stage people feel 'in a vacuum'. Marjorie's need to 'hide' lessens as she recognises its source, but she does not yet feel confident about how to behave and be herself as she begins to emerge.

This stage of letting go one way of being, before taking up another, has in its turn to be recognised and accepted as part of the experience of changing.

Once people have become determined to look and to observe themselves, many people have said that they have never found anything more intriguing than discovering their own 'sabotaging' abilities. It is important not to underestimate the depth of the effort that is involved for some in achieving change in themselves. The struggle is often experienced as immense, and often it feels *toughest of all at the point when it is nearly over*. When the 'resistance' is nearly 'overcome' it seems to hold its greatest power! It is vital for people engaged in therapy to know this. The therapist needs to sustain the client during this time by sharing the knowledge gained from experience. The therapist must explain that the harshest resistance is coming only because the client has moved to the stage where they dare to challenge their earlier beliefs most strongly.

## The importance of 'transference'

'Transference' is a word originally used by analytical therapists. It means in ordinary language that one puts upon, or 'transfers', feelings about someone that originated with someone else. It is not a strange or mysterious event that only happens in therapy.

We are all doing it all the time. Every time we meet someone we immediately like and feel comfortable with, or we instantly dislike even before we know them, the reasons for such feelings are to do with previous encounters. Most of us are quick to move from the particular 'one-off' experience to a general view. 'I don't like redhaired women', was a comment made recently. One might be tempted to ask how many redhaired women this man had met! More importantly, questions needed to be asked so that he could perhaps recall the pain, fear or humiliation experienced long ago at the hands of a redhaired woman.

'I don't like fat men', was a similar comment which quickly led to a woman talking about her boss. Later, the connection was to a 'beer belly' and memories of waiting for her father to return home from the pub with a frighteningly unpredictable temper.

These feelings, emphatically expressed by people, can spring from one unpleasant or fearful memory, but are most likely to arise from experiences that cannot be recalled at all.

'Transference' is so valuable in therapy because the client will inevitably bring old feelings and old patterns of behaviour into the relationship with the therapist. These frequently consist of fears about feeling unacceptable, unloved or rejected in some way by the therapist, because these are such common experiences in early life and in relation to parents. As a result clients test their therapists again and again by being late or by making demands in order to see where the 'boundaries' are set in the relationship. Louise Eichenbaum and Susie Orbach (1985) have written about how particularly hard it is for women to know where boundaries are in their relationships. They will often hold back their needs in therapy, because of the ingrained teaching that they have had about looking after others. As a result, many women clients spend a lot of energy 'looking after' the therapist.

Because the client is not going to be feeling or behaving radically differently in the therapy sessions from how they behave outside, they will inevitably act out, sometimes at a very painful level, the same conflicts that they have been struggling with all their lives. Their 'neurotic solutions' come to the fore in the same way in their relationship with the therapist. Someone may believe that if they dare to express what they want they are doomed not to have it. This can make such a person appear either casual about therapy, make them silent in it, or feel very angry and fearful about the therapist's power to give it or withhold it. Such feelings are then available to be examined and understood, often for the very first time by the client in a safe and caring atmosphere.

Some therapists deny the huge effect that their going on holiday, terminating their posts or ending a client's therapy abruptly can have on their clients. I believe that such a view denies the importance of the therapy relationship and all that the client builds into it, whenever work of real depth has been engaged in.

This leads to the equally important matter of the therapist 'transferring' feelings on to the client. This was called 'counter-transference' by Freud. One hopes that all counsellors and therapists have done sufficient work on understanding themselves to be at least alert to these feelings, and not inadvertently to abuse their clients. Unfortunately, some clients have experienced their therapist's need to be 'all powerful' even to the lengths of experiencing sexual abuse by them. Dr. Masters and Johnson (1970) referred to this when they made their study of human sexual behaviour in the USA. They were shocked and saddened to hear that it was not all that unusual for women clients to have had sexual encounters with male therapists. They describe these incidents as 'tragic' and put them in the category of 'therapeutic failure'.

It is not uncommon for clients to hold deep love feelings for their therapist and sometimes sexual desires towards them. I believe the therapist needs to view such feelings with deep sensitivity and respect and holds full responsibility not to act on them. They need to be brought out into the open and explored. Often such feelings can be rejoiced at, for they generally arise in people who have no outlet for them in their lives elsewhere, yet have a deep desire to be sexual. Such loving sexual feelings should never be mocked or ridiculed but an understanding of them needs to be sought instead. It is probable that such feelings or fantasies can only be experienced by the client because he or she knows it is 'safe', and 'not available' in reality and that the therapist will control it. It is often a compulsively repeated experience that the client has felt from the past of 'unrequited' love with their own parent. Seeking 'impossible' love from a source where once again it will not be available, the client relives the early feelings of deprivation, frustration and anger and demonstrates the 'old' position of feeling 'unwanted' or 'not worthy'.

## The three stages of therapy

If one examines therapy of the kind that occurs weekly or more frequently over a period of two or more years, and carried out in what is described as a psycho-dynamic way, it generally seems to fall into three stages. These do not end or change in a clear-cut way; rather, the client and therapist move through them together, with the client recognising the second and the third stages mainly by looking back and comparing them with the first.

The first consists of the client talking about the 'trigger' event – what has happened to them *now* that has led to the request for therapy. They may be feeling particularly distressed – crying, unable to go to work, perhaps feeling particularly upset about a relationship. Their current story with all its complicated aspects begins to be told and they slowly recognise the conflict that exists between what they wish for, and how thwarted they are in achieving it.

This 'story-telling' in the first stage gradually merges into a second stage, which consists of recognising the *source* of the beliefs. For example, *why* Marjorie felt compelled to hide, and how painful this was. Anthony recognised that he had chosen to be 'sick' rather than take promotion. Rosemary feared 'going mad' as her boyfriend simultaneously promised great love to her but spoke of being obsessed with another woman.

The second stage of therapy is characterised by the client's gradual understanding that their feelings and the perceptions they hold of themselves stem from experiences gained in their early life. The 'solutions' they have felt driven to carry out over and over again have not worked to solve their conflicts. Moreover the perceptions are seen as false ones. Margaret is *not* responsible for her father's death, nor is it necessary for Jim to deny his adult sexuality by creating his 'tiny penis'. This is a time of dawning recognition that the 'old patterns' might be altered or loosened, that *perhaps* a different perception of self could be found. Out of this recognition comes a massive amount of emotion. It may be overwhelming sadness or anger or a mixture of the two. A deep sense of loss, like mourning, occurs over the 'time wasted', as the client recognises how the distorted view of self has led to their continuing a version of the early deprivation in their family. Anthony experiences deep pain at not having been able to rejoice in his abilities during his earlier years. Regret and sadness play a large part for many people in this second stage. It can be used as a block to continuing therapy. It can also be used to motivate even more strongly the feeling that no more time is to be wasted on 'old ways' of behaving, and an urgency is felt to take risks with new ways despite knowing that the worst possible 'backlash' may occur.

The third stage begins when the client actually moves out to act and behave *differently* in a situation where he or she would previously have applied the 'neurotic solution' (that is, to feel they must withdraw and hide, or resentfully to 'take care' of someone or to deny their own value and abilities). The effort involved in *'playing it differently'* is immense at first, and often the 'sabotage' at this stage takes a very complicated form. For example, a job may be sought and the person feels they are moving towards it in a good way, but it is a job doomed to fail. Perhaps a relationship is formed that is only repeating the old experience of being inappropriate or not really available. The agony is experienced yet again, but this time the person *sees* it, and instead of feeling crushed and hopeless the 'sabotage' of themselves has been *recognised* and they feel determined to try again.

In a sense the third stage lasts for the rest of the person's life, for they take responsibility for their own therapy. They need to stay with the therapist long enough to try out and experience a different way of being until they feel the new way is experienced as their *real* self. The swing has occurred from the old ways of the compulsive 'neurotic solution' dominating their life, to a new way of feeling and behaving. The person at the start of the third stage feels a bit fragile but is, for example, out of hiding and operating as they want to. They can validate themselves without believing this can only be provided by others. They can now hold on to real achievements, no longer believing that this will lead to harming others or will bring fearful rejection of themselves.

The old ways of feeling and behaviour may occur occasionally even many years after therapy has ended, but the person will recognise them and no longer be crushed by it. It is seen as a little 'echo' from the past and makes them fully aware of how much they have taken their 'new self' for granted.

# 6 The Body's Expression of Conflict

In the previous chapter the connection between 'mental pain' and bodily pain was described in terms of how our feelings are experienced in our bodies. This chapter attempts to show how sometimes we have quite severe physical complaints or symptoms which express our feelings. Such feelings are generally ones that we are fearful of acknowledging because they would then give us 'mental pain', yet it seems that they cannot be denied or completely hidden. As a result they are 'acted out' in a variety of ways by our bodies, and this process allows our expression of them while simultaneously hiding both the feelings and the meaning of them from ourselves.

The word 'psychosomatic' is used by doctors to describe such complaints or symptoms when they believe that their cause is more to do with the person's feelings about the situation that they are in, rather than any infection or injury.

In the past, when most people had little access to medical knowledge or information about their bodies, these sorts of psychosomatic conditions were sometimes displayed in a very startling and rather simplistic way. For example, people rather dramatically 'could not see', or were suddenly 'unable to walk' or had paralysis of an arm. Some of the doctors who were later to become the early psychoanalysts showed how under hypnosis such 'patients' could move their 'paralysed' limbs and a great interest became focused on the power of the 'mind over body'. Today it is rare to find such simplistic forms of psychosomatic conditions, but there are very many more complicated forms which I believe require a great deal of unravelling in order to be understood.

In one sense the word 'psychosomatic' is strangely meaningless, because we are all 'mind' and 'body' all the time. As explained in the previous chapter, none of us experience feelings without also knowing of them through bodily sensations. The opposite is also true, for nobody who experiences severe pain, illness or any restriction of their body, can do this without some emotional response.

The idea that our bodies express our feelings is so well understood that it is commonly expressed in everyday language. How often someone who is annoying us is not only felt to be, but is actually described as, 'a pain in the neck' or a 'headache'. Recently the term 'scabs' was used as a description of one group of workers by another. This language shows just how aware we are that certain feelings lead to bodily sensations, as well as how badly we feel about certain diseases and the stigma attached to them.

People in the modern western world have been taught to think of disease largely in terms of infection or of organic deterioration or trauma (that is, our bodies wearing out or being injured). This implies that all these things 'happen' to our bodies and have very little to do with what is going on in our minds. This view of illness has of course a huge rational and scientific body of evidence to support it, but it has led to many people believing that the only reason that they become ill, or have symptoms, is because of occurrences outside themselves.

It is only relatively recently that medical researchers have given much more attention to the part our resistance to disease plays in keeping us healthy. The part of our body that helps us to fight infections is known as the immune system. Perhaps, in the future, less attention will be given to drugs to fight individual infections and far more will be concentrated on learning how to improve our immune systems as a way of preventing many different kinds of illness. This may be one possible positive development to come out of the otherwise horrifying spread of AIDS.

When a doctor, or even a friend, suggests to any of us that the symptoms or complaints that we suffer from could be 'psychosomatic', we tend to stiffen, to feel 'on the defensive', and in some sense criticised. Such a suggestion is often felt to imply that the symptoms are 'imagined', that we are 'putting them on', that we are ill 'for our own ends'; this tends to make us feel guilty and angry.

Many writers have attempted to explain psychosomatic symptoms, but none in my view does so as clearly as Dr Kübler Ross, who wrote: 'Physical discomforts are a means of alleviating guilt feelings for suppressed hostile wishes' (1973). In other words, because we seem ready to feel guilty whenever we are angry or resentful (especially women in our society), instead of openly expressing these feelings and risking the rejection they could bring we 'bury' or deny the resentment or anger and deal with the guilt by suffering, thereby punishing ourselves for it with pain.

Dr Kübler Ross goes on to say that it is surprising how a simple interview can often reveal these feelings. Sometimes a few explanations and reassurance that feelings of love *and hate* are human and understandable and do not require the 'gruesome price' of pain, can lessen the symptoms.

When we start to examine psychosomatic conditions it is apparent that they operate as another form of 'neurotic solution' – perhaps they are one of the most common of all. They too provide no opportunity for *resolution* of the conflict; instead they protect us from knowledge of it. Two stories are illustrative of people whose symptoms protected them from recognising hidden aspects of themselves. Peter's fear of being angry and damaging others was turned around on to himself, so he was 'ill' rather than risk standing up for himself and getting the feared retaliation. Hilary felt she had to control herself with superb efficiency, so that the 'messy', out of control part of herself was forced to be expressed in the form of an 'illness'. One extreme feeling led to the forced expression of its opposite.

Peter's history showed that he had experienced a great deal of distress in his childhood when his parents rowed constantly, behaved violently and threatened to separate. He grew up fearful of expressing any anger, or any needs of his own. He had married a woman who had herself been so seriously ill that Peter thought she was going to die. Caring for her had both frightened and exhausted him. When she recovered he greatly feared becoming ill himself. He experienced her as angry that he was moving into 'her territory', and there was no space for him to be ill, weak or cared for, even after a long period of caring for her.

Peter felt unable to stake a claim for himself, or to express his own needs for fear of upsetting her. The more unreasonable he felt her demands to be, the more he 'crumpled up' and was unable to make a stand for himself. He began to see that he used being 'ill' as a protection from expressing anger that he felt could be as destructive as his parents' anger had seemed to him as a child. He was slowly able to separate out his wife's fears of the world and her expectations of rejection from his own feelings. He began to take a calmer, more assertive line; neither oppressive of her, nor being oppressed by her. His sweats and shakes lessened, and he gradually stopped taking tranquillizers. He put it clearly when he described himself as 'better, because he no longer had to be "ill", if there was "hassle"'.

Hilary was a very business-like and efficient woman, who suffered from rectal bleeding and unpredictable diarrhoea. She had come to the conclusion that her severe colitis might have a psychological aspect to it, because it was so much worse when she felt under stress. When she started therapy she was trying to prove that she was 'as good as any man'. She felt that her brother had always been given greater value by the family than herself.

In an effort to be super-efficient, clean, tidy and correct in every way, it was paradoxical that her symptoms were dirty, explosive and embarrassing, making her feel out of control and very vulnerable. She was determined not to become pregnant or even to have periods, which she was controlling by remaining continuously on an oral contraceptive.

She worked very hard, and rather despised many of her colleagues. As she spoke about her childhood, she began to recognise that these negative feelings about others were really a protection which covered a deep fear of being rejected herself. She sought approval endlessly, particularly from her father who long ago had hit her when some menstrual blood had shown on her clothes.

Hilary decided to come off the 'pill', and she began to recognise that all the steps she took to 'prove' herself 'better' than men were only a clear demonstration of her own doubts. Her real 'breakthrough' came when she made friends with a woman whom she later invited to stay with her. She had never had a close woman friend before. To discover she was 'likeable' had a profound effect, and she realised that she could like herself and did not have to 'prove' anything. The bleeding gradually ceased, and a year after therapy ended she took up horse-riding and even enjoyed jumping.

This seemed the strongest evidence of her own belief that she was completely clear of symptoms!

Hilary seemed to have been expressing both her anger and her pain over her feelings of being rejected because she was female. She felt that her envy towards men had to be strongly controlled, yet the resentment was expressed through her symptoms. As she experienced greater acceptance of herself, and found that this was available, so her envy and fear lessened and her symptoms cleared.

There is one very common psychosomatic condition that affects women. They generally first consult their GPs about it, but it is also the commonest reason for referral to gynaecological out-patients. The symptoms are pain, soreness, burning, irritation and itching of the vulva or vagina, and sometimes an excessive discharge. Women find it very distressing and embarrassing. It can be so severe at times that it is uncomfortable to walk or even sit down.

This is a condition that is so frequently mis-diagnosed and misunderstood that I make no apology about using the remainder of this chapter to describe the condition in detail, as it holds all the elements common to other psychosomatic complaints and shows the value of psychotherapy as a method of treatment. Women also need to be able to recognise this condition and to request both proper testing and further help in understanding how to free themselves of it.

A few years ago, when I was working at Birmingham Brook Advisory Centre, I was able to use DHSS funding to make a research study of psychosomatic vaginitis, because infection testing clinics had been set up in the Centre as part of an improved contraceptive service. Women came to the clinic with symptoms of vaginal pain, soreness or severe itching. They were carefully examined and full swabs were taken, and when any infection was found they were always prescribed the appropriate treatment.

Quite soon, however, it became apparent that a number of women left the clinic feeling annoyed and bewildered. In spite of very careful examination their swabs showed no infection and they were told there was 'nothing the matter'. For many of these women their symptoms had been going on for years. As they talked with the doctor their stories always followed the same pattern. They had sought help from a number of different doctors and had been given a great deal of chemo-therapy, mostly in the form of anti-fungal pessaries or antibiotic pills, but their symptoms had persisted.

The study was set up to see if a different, more effective form of treatment could be found and these women were offered a chance to talk about themselves. A few refused and felt angry at the implication that any psychological aspects might be involved. Others, however, were in a state of despair and were 'ready to try anything'. They came to talk and eventually began to think differently. The first hurdle for these women to overcome was to accept that reliable tests had been done. This required time given to looking together at the bacteriologists' notes, and to understand the seemingly mysterious information on the swab reports.

Such a simple and obvious way of helping these women to feel a part of the process was sadly a rare experience for them in a clinical setting. It had an important effect in preventing them from feeling 'fobbed off', as it were, with statements that they could neither question nor properly understand. This kind of experience had previously been a common one for so many of them. Once they could accept that they did not have an infection, they could move on to recognising that they did have a condition and, moreover, one that was real. No-one was suggesting that their symptoms were imagined. In fact, it was necessary to emphasise that in many ways their condition was more painful and more stressful than an infection, because infections generally respond quite quickly to the correct treatment. The unpleasant aspect of a psychosomatic condition is the difficulty in finding quick relief for the symptoms.

The second hurdle was much harder to overcome and took longer to achieve. This consisted of helping the person to look at and to discover for themselves how and why the condition had started in the first place. Also, why it persisted when to all intents and purposes the person who had it was suffering and apparently wanted to be rid of it.

Once the women began to examine the patterns of their symptoms, clues appeared about the aspects of their lives that were the source of deeper conflicts and distress which they had not previously felt able to examine or recognise. As they talked, the women realised that for some the pain and irritation started up as soon as they came home from holiday. For another it was in the middle of the night, and yet another only at weekends. This kind of recognition enabled the women to see for themselves that this is not the way infections usually show themselves. It also led the woman concerned to ask herself questions about her feelings at these particular times and specially to think about who she was with, or about to meet, when the pain or irritation was severe.

Joyce, aged 20, suffered from constant vaginal irritation and soreness. She wanted to have a sex life with her boyfriend. However, to do this meant to go completely against the views of her parents who strongly disapproved (and with whom she lived). Joyce found a 'solution' to this conflict by agreeing to be sexual with her boyfriend. But in reality she was unable to do so because of intense vaginal soreness, which enabled her to say 'no' to sex for an apparently justifiable reason. Sometimes one's body really can 'speak', and in a startlingly clear way Joyce's body was expressing her view that it really did 'hurt' to be sexual in a situation of such parental opposition. The burning pain also expressed the feelings of resentment she experienced about the position she was in. She expressed a sense of guilt about 'depriving' her boyfriend as she put it, but said her symptoms meant that she too was deprived. Either way Joyce feared rejection, for to be 'sexual' meant risking parental rejection and if she was not sexual with her boyfriend she also feared his rejection.

Girls are heavily pressurised from a very early age to 'please' people, and Joyce was caught in a situation where she could not 'please' both her parents and her boyfriend. She also felt very uncertain about how to 'please' herself.

As this example shows, psychosomatic conditions always offer some form of 'solution' to a situation or problem which the person had adopted. Like the other 'neurotic solutions' already described, the 'price' to be paid for such 'solutions' generally includes a high level of suffering. All the women with vaginitis who joined in the study experienced a struggle as they began to realise that part of them wanted to be free of the condition, but another part did not want to examine the role their symptoms were playing in 'solving' their conflict. To recognise this was to risk not being able to 'use' their symptoms any more, and having their conflict exposed. It was always from conflict that the vaginitis, albeit temporarily, had in some sense 'rescued' them.

At the end of the research study some of the women involved in it agreed to write about their feelings. For anyone who has never had a long-term vaginitis it is hard to appreciate how distressing it can be. One woman wrote as follows: 'I have suffered, and I really do mean suffered, embarrassment, pain, desperation from which I now know to be vaginitis for approximately eight or nine years.' Another wrote: 'I have carried so much anxiety, discomfort and even anguish over the years I've had my problem with vaginitis.'

Sometimes, because of the failure of the condition to respond to chemical treatments, some women feared that they had something seriously wrong. One woman wrote: 'I suffered from itching and soreness, yes, and as a library assistant spent many a lunch hour poring over medical dictionaries convinced that I had some rare disease.'

Some women felt bewildered by the doctor's lack of explanation. One wrote of her experiences after visiting a Special Clinic in a hospital: 'They found nothing, so I went away feeling, well, I have not got anything wrong with me, they have proved that – but I know I *have* got something wrong with me – have they missed it, etc.? The result of this was total bewilderment, and visit number two a year or so later, of course, with the same result.'

In the study emphasis was all the time placed on helping each woman try and understand what their condition was about, why they had particular symptoms at certain times and when these had started and what seemed to make them recur. One woman wrote:

At first, I totally rejected the idea that my physical problems were associated with my psychological ones. I felt that if this were the case I ought to be able to will them to go away and I could not. I took a lot of convincing and in the end it was by resolving my problems which in my case meant having the confidence to take control of my own life, that I conquered it.

Another woman described her experiences in this way:

After being unsuccessfully treated at my doctor's he referred me to a specialist, who duly treated me for an infection, and he gave my husband treatment too. He also did several fertility tests for both of us as we had been trying for a family for four years. He later wrote to inform us that there was nothing seriously wrong and he could do no more. I felt completely dejected as my husband and I still had symptoms of the infection. I then came to the Infection Testing Clinic convinced that it could not be just imagination. After the tests there, it was proved that I was in fact clear. I then had two sessions with a counsellor and my vaginitis and the rash my husband had been suffering from disappeared. Four months later I became pregnant, which I feel sure would never have happened if no-one had taken the trouble to listen, understand and advise me.

Each situation that these women described held some feelings of resentment or anger that they had previously felt unable to recognise or express. Once it could be carefully, slowly and accurately described and shared, and the accompanying guilt seen as totally unjustified, the symptoms often disappeared with surprising rapidity.

One of the most convincing experiences for the women was to have their symptoms reappear, and for the person concerned to understand why. One woman, for example, recalled how astonished she felt when her symptoms suddenly returned when she felt angry with her husband. Recognition of the connection between the two incidents convinced her of the psychological origin of her vaginitis.

One woman told a complicated story of having suffered from 'endogenous depression', for which she had had drug treatment from a psychiatrist. She came to the clinic very worried about her painful vaginitis which was not responding to chemo-therapy, and as it was causing her such distress she feared a return of the so called 'endogenous' depression. This diagnosis defines the depression as coming from *within* the person and not caused by any outside event or experience. I do not believe such a form of depression exists, but understandably this description frightened her. As she talked it seemed to her that her symptoms were worse on Wednesdays. When this rather startling view was examined more closely, it seemed that this was the day in the week which she associated with the start of her periods. When asked what she felt about them she said, 'Just one more egg gone'.

It soon became clear that she felt huge pressure to marry and to become pregnant, neither of which at that point she wanted. She was an adopted child and her only brother, who had had two little girls, had recently had a vasectomy. This left the woman feeling that she carried sole responsibility to produce a 'son' for her adoptive mother, who had been unable to have children of her own.

Once these feelings were talked about and the woman was able to believe in her own right to conduct her life as she wanted, the vaginitis not only went away, but so did the depression. A follow-up contact some three years later found her well and with an enjoyable sex life.

Another young woman came for counselling with her husband because she had such pain on intercourse that they were no longer making love in ways that she and her husband perceived as 'normal'. She had had some very unpleasant procedures carried out, including cauterising her cervix and widening the opening of the urethra, all in the name of 'improving' her vaginitis. The pain, however, remained unchanged.

When she started to talk, it became clear that she had always experienced her vagina like a 'wound'. Having previously been advised by a doctor to practise inserting a finger into her vagina in order to get used to the sensation of containing a penis, she understandably asked, 'How can I stick my finger into a hole that feels like that?' She also told of how she had been brought up in a family where all talk of sex was avoided. The occasional mention indicated that sex was disgusting, and she had not previously felt able even to look at her genitals.

In spite of this she enjoyed oral sex and was able to reach a climax; severe pain only occurred on penetration. She began to talk about how difficult she felt it was to say 'no', and also to ask for what *she* wanted. It was also difficult to share these fears openly with her husband, even though he was an exceptionally understanding and sensitive person. She also realised that her expectation of pain played a part in making it occur, but soon discovered she was able to control it. She had intercourse free of pain, but once this occurred she was inevitably afraid to try again as she was convinced the pain would recur. She tried again, and found that provided she determined when intercourse occurred there was no pain. She then started to feel guilty about 'controlling' their love-making in this way. A real 'breakthrough' came when they bought a vibrator which she wanted, and she realised she could have sex as she determined it without having to feel that she had to 'please' or feel resentful.

The results of the study into psychosomatic vaginitis are written up elsewhere (Woodward, 1981). It was interesting and encouraging to find that given an opportunity to talk and to explore their feelings in a friendly, informal setting, 87 per cent of the women in the study recorded themselves free of symptoms or 'improved' at a six month follow-up interview with a doctor not involved with the treatment. From my short time in a Special Clinic I feel convinced that men suffer from an equivalent condition for quite different reasons. Such research awaits investigation by someone else.

**Why is psychosomatic vaginitis so common?**

It is difficult to produce 'hard' evidence about why so many women suffer from vaginitis, but it is easy to make suggestions! For women this part of their body is the one where so many significant, intense and emotional events are experienced. These are menstruation, sex, followed by contraception, in some instances pregnancy, birth, abortion and menopause. It is an area which gives us very intense joy and pain. Because of parental attitudes, as well as those in society, many women experience great frustration about the under-valuing, even denial, of their sexuality, which can lead to the resentment expressed through vaginitis.

Boys and girls are given such opposing messages about sex. Boys, by and large, have 'permission' to be sexual; yet girls are strongly discouraged, except in strangely disguised forms. There is not even a word in the English language to describe a normal, healthy, sexual female! All words describe women as either sexually 'bad', 'mad' or 'incompetent' (the whore, the nymphomaniac or the 'frigid'). Only sexual intercourse is defined as 'proper sex', which gives the man stimulus leading to arousal. A man will often attempt to recreate this for himself when masturbating, by cupping his hand around the penis and moving it. Women rarely simulate intercourse when masturbating.

Intercourse with full penetration exposes women to the greatest risk of pregnancy and, as Shere Hite's (1976) research showed, it often does not arouse women, because for many of them penetration does not produce the stimulation that leads to orgasm. Often oral or manual stimulation of the clitoris is seen as 'second best'. Women have often described how obliged they feel to please their partners, yet fearful of 'boring' them by asking for their own needs to be met.

When equal value is given to sex in ways that women also want, their ability to be sexual and to have multiple orgasms physiologically far outstrips the male's capacity to be sexual, because his orgasm involves ejaculation followed by an enforced period of rest.

Perhaps this is one of the reasons why many men have needed to define 'sex' as something they want on *their* terms, rather than as a truly joint activity with the needs of both partners being given equal value with both obtaining equal pleasure. It may also be one of the reasons why some men are so threatened by the idea of lesbian love-making.

## Seeking medical advice

Unfortunately women often experience being 'dismissed' by their doctors when they go to their surgeries with complaints that are specifically female ones, such as pre-menstrual tension or menopausal symptoms. They sometimes feel that they are not given the same attention that would be offered to male patients, and feel afraid of being unable to 'please' the doctor if their symptoms are not rapidly 'cured'. We can all make an important contribution to our own health by seeing if we can understand any pain or symptoms that arise. It is of utmost importance to have persistent symptoms properly checked and to query if there is an organic cause as far as can reasonably be known. It is always helpful to keep a diary of when and how persistent or troublesome symptoms occur. It is specially valuable to be aware of the thoughts and feelings that come to mind if a specific symptom recurs. We are all familiar with the notion of being 'allergic to Mondays', but many people suffer from conditions such as attacks of diarrhoea before going away from home. If such conditions seem to follow a strange pattern we can examine this and try to understand for ourselves if they seem to be providing 'a solution' to a situation that we are in. If we can discover what this is, we may be able to perceive alternative or better 'solutions' for ourselves, or to seek help with counsellors or therapists to help us do so.

# 7 The Experience of Psychotherapy

Many therapists have written about their views on psychotherapy, but it is relatively rare to hear of the experience of psychotherapy from the client's point of view.

I believe it is particularly difficult for clients to write about therapy, because it is a complicated process in which they are very deeply involved. The important changes that occur consist of the person recognising aspects of themselves that were previously not understood. Much of 'how they were' slowly sinks out of their awareness and is 'forgotten'. How they 'used to feel' has become dim at best, and understandably there is generally no wish to recall it.

In spite of this fact, five people who experienced therapy volunteered to write about it, and I am very grateful to them. The reason for doing so was to share with others how it felt for them. The accounts have not been produced as 'voyeuristic' experiences, but in order to help de-mystify the therapeutic process for the benefit of other people's understanding; particularly for anyone thinking of embarking on psychotherapy for themselves.

Because it is so difficult to write about this type of experience, I suggested some headings to them that would make a chronological framework if they felt like using them.

1 The symptoms, and the feelings you had about them that led you to seek therapy.
2 Any previous 'treatment' and your feelings about that.
3 Your attitude and expectations about psychotherapy prior to embarking on it.
4 Your experience of the therapy sessions.
5 Comments about any changes you have experienced.

6 Your current position; and whether you would advise others to seek therapy or to avoid it.

The first four have used this framework in their own way, and the last one wrote an account of her response to a small number of therapy sessions focused on a specific problem.

## Account 1: Margaret's experience of psychotherapy

*The symptoms and the feelings I had about them that led me to seek therapy*

I had a feeling of being pushed or pulled into situations that I couldn't handle. It seemed that for most of my life people had been pushing or pulling me into ways I did not want to go. (For example, my mother's ambition was for me to be a teacher.)

I felt desperate; as if trapped into behaving in certain ways, and then felt very resentful. I was nice and kind to people, and yet with some of them I was saying to myself, 'Leave me alone; keep out of my way'.

I felt quite inadequate to deal with what life seemed to be piling up on me in certain areas, and at work I refused to believe that I was any good.

I felt jealous of women my husband came into contact with for fear of losing him. I was waking up in the night, not able to go back to sleep, which felt like an enforced being alone.

I kept finding myself in a muddle and felt the 'dope' of the family – quite ridiculous, and asked 'Why can't I get it right?'. It felt as if I had no ability to apply my intelligence.

*Previous 'treatment', if any, and feelings about that*

I am thinking back to the time when I was 22 and gave up teaching because I had a kind of breakdown. My mother took me to a homeopathic doctor and I can remember taking little white pills. Quite soon afterwards she took me to a woman doctor at a medical centre. I only remember going once, and I don't remember what she said, but I have a feeling that it was she who let me off the hook (i.e. enabled my mother to accept that teaching was the wrong place for me).

Some years later I had about eighteen months' counselling at a child guidance clinic because of my son's aggressive behaviour at nursery school. I definitely felt a failure having to go there.

It was hard to get there as I also had a baby of eighteen months. I wanted to go and get a lot of help, and I looked on the counsellor as a kind of saviour. We talked about my mother's background, and I can remember crying about my father's death. I did see at that time that it wasn't 'my fault', but the 'keeping alive' thing didn't emerge. I have often thought that if it hadn't been for her, my son would have grown up delinquent. It has just occurred to me that this is the real reason for the five year gap between my two daughters – I didn't feel adequate.

## Your attitude and expectations about psychotherapy prior to embarking on it

When I went to the person at the medical centre, I felt helpless and useless – taken by my mother who was very concerned about me, but I had no expectations.

Going to the child guidance clinic, I felt thankful that there was someone who would help – I was feeling the 'odd one out', but have since used it to encourage people to seek that kind of help. At the time I had no idea what might happen.

With the psychotherapy that I am writing about, I knew of the therapist, and thought from my knowledge of her that she was able to be open and honest – something I don't think I could be often, although I tried desperately hard at a certain kind of honesty. So I saw her as someone with whom it would be easier to make a start. My expectations were nil. No! – I knew that I would cry a lot. I knew I was in a muddle, and saw the therapist as helping me to sort it out.

## My experience of the psychotherapy sessions

I valued the consistently warm friendly welcome and start. Our acquaintanceship was always acknowledged with just the right touch. Sometimes we talked a bit about family matters, sometimes we just got going, and the comfortable sense of order felt right for me.

The crying was uncomfortable, but essential for me. I actually found myself starting on the way there, because there was something I desperately needed to cry about. It was a relief to know that I could cry there, and to be able to say exactly what I was thinking and feeling. I felt fear that I wouldn't be able to get things 'right', for myself as I wanted them to be, or remember what the therapist said, or that I would miss something that would help me to make it work. This had to be lived through until I saw that sometimes I could get it 'right' and sometimes couldn't. I realised that I could only hold onto bits of what the therapist said, but I knew I could always go back and go over it again.

The therapist warned me that I might feel angry with her and I found that helpful. I couldn't imagine that I would, and I didn't! I wonder if I had gone through that with the counsellor at child guidance because I remember I was supposed not to get cross with my son! Once he did something which made me angry, and I smacked his leg and shouted, 'damn that woman'! (the counsellor).

The psychotherapy sessions always had a sense of momentum. I always had a lot to say, and the therapist moved me on. I had a sense of her expertise in doing this consistently, and it gave me something firm to work with. I came away and applied what I had learned through more understanding of myself and people and situations that I encountered.

Sometimes I got bits of it 'right', and it felt marvellous – in control but gently so. If it didn't go 'right', I knew I'd have another chance before long. It was my control – not somebody else's.

The sessions never felt distorted, because the material always came from me. The therapist just worked with it. I liked the idea that she was the 'mirror' and valued the practical suggestions about possible ways of responding.

I have dumped sacks full of guilt and fear and frustration on the therapist's floor, and they have melted away!

I found the sessions were as open as I could possibly want. For years I have read words about philosophies and religion, and attempted to make the words work for me. They have been

like a sort of crust – a way of having a good image of the world –
to cover up the 'bad fairy' which I thought of as the real me. I
can now do without those words. I can look at them and take
them or leave them as I please. I don't have to hang on to them
in order to survive.

My major emotions were relief, tremendous anger focused at
first on a very demanding neighbour because I couldn't cope
with her, and also on other people. I felt elation at being able
to change, and some aggression towards my husband, but being
able to say to him 'please understand – I'll get through this bit'
and then joy when he could, and finding that our relationship
has been so enriched. Feeling now confident – though not
always!

### Comments about changes I experienced

I recall talking twice about dreams. I might have brought them
in more with hindsight, although I can see now what connection
they had with my sense of 'muddle', so perhaps I didn't find it
necessary. I had dreamed of a black cat biting my hand and
hanging on while I tried to shake it off. I also dreamed of the
class that ran amok and the exam that I hadn't a hope of passing
because I didn't know anything.

I had many memories of things that had gone wrong – all the
'bad bits', and recalled the anguish I felt as a little child. Being
able to go through those feelings again and to come out the
other side still intact with the therapist there to support me by
listening and helping me, led me to find the next positive step.

I didn't know that what I was doing was trying to keep
everybody alive. It was instinctive and compulsive. I was amazed
to discover it, and to think about its implications. I was surprised
to find myself able to believe the therapist's positive thoughts
about me. Apart from the family, by whom I do feel loved, it
had never occurred to me that people would like me, or to think
why they seek my company. I had a poor self image. Now I
think more about and of myself which I know makes me a better
person, and I don't bother or care really what other people
think about me. I'm surprised about that. I experienced (and of
course am going on, and probably always will) having to think
very hard indeed about what is going on around me. I am having

to hold back and decide what, if anything, I am going to do or say about it. I fall into the same old 'trap', but I am gradually getting some of the 'hooks' out! I notice that nobody seems to think any the worse of me for it, and I continue to get feedback from my daughters when they see me not keeping them or somebody else alive, and they praise me for it!

My husband seems much more relaxed and contented and able to choose what he wants to do more. I am much more honest with him. He has always been honest with me. *For the first time in my life I understand what I am doing.*

## Current position

I am very glad that I started on psychotherapy. I am not at all regretful, and would strongly advise other people to do it and have done so! There is nothing to lose, and even if one doesn't find the right person first time, that doesn't mean one should just give up. Several times over the 25 years between going to the child guidance clinic and to the therapist, I thought about going back to the child guidance counsellor, but somehow never did. I suppose I thought I ought to be able to get things right for myself, or that other people had a greater need. In 1970, I took on some different religious beliefs as a way of looking good to the world, but they have never taken a very large part in my life, and are now only fairly superficial activities which suit me in some kind of way.

## Gain or loss

I requested notes from the therapist for me early on – at a guess perhaps after the third session – and I found them very helpful. They showed me the 'old base' and the 'new'. At the time the gains the therapist suggested I could look for – freedom, peace, time and cohesion – seemed quite unattainable but gradually I saw that they were all becoming realities. I do feel a sense of freedom. I don't need to barrack myself in the back bedroom, daring anybody to come and make demands on me. I do feel more peaceful. I don't find myself saying, 'Why the hell doesn't she go to someone else for help – I can't cope with her'. People seem to be learning not to make so many demands on me. I do have more time to myself and I love it. I do feel a sense of cohesion. In a difficult patch recently, I found myself able to use my head and my heart (by which I suppose I mean my whole self), to work through it. I never once thought about religion.

## Loss

I have lost some of my sense of power. I used to panic when I saw power available to me almost as though I was being pushed into being powerful (e.g. I begged the Headmistress not to make me Head Prefect, and was dismayed when she refused. I had no sense of pride, just anguish that I would get it all wrong). This is going to take a lot of getting rid of, but it involves extreme diligence at holding back from keeping people alive – though great fun to practice it!

The habitual way of behaving has the same feeling about it as the power – slow to go but definitely changing. I am finding a more natural easy response to people and situations and seem better able to control what I'm doing without being afraid of upsetting or annoying or turning people away from me.

The 'gains' have a greater impetus. I suppose I hang on to the losses.

## The effect on symptoms and my present life

I'm beginning to feel more of a person. I think I'm more aware in an honest real way of other people. We touch each others' lives and their life goes on and we move on. It's not such a heavy business. I feel lighter of heart and sometimes it's hard and sometimes I'm sad, but I can see better what is happening to me. I am leaving my job in education. I know now that some bits of it I'm quite good at, but I don't want to do it. I have decided to take more responsibility for the garden, which is a relief to my husband. I am learning to control my store cupboard of knowledge and experience. I am much clearer about how to manage my evening classes. I don't need to keep all my students alive now!

Looking back through my notes, I realise how preoccupied I was with my neighbour. It was her turning to me that caused me to seek help. Her tragedy on top of all her problems was quite beyond my help. It was her husband's death that was the link with my father's.

Looking back at the 'symptoms' I listed at the beginning of this account, they have gone! – in the main – of course I expect the old patterns to rear up from time to time, but I know I can't go back to that awful *muddle!*

When I decided that I wanted to be 'let out on a long life-line' I felt a sense of elation at striking out alone – yet knowing that I could go back to the therapist at any time – as indeed I did once, and know that I may feel I want to again.

I know that I'm pretty slow at re-shaping my life, but it's coming and I feel that I've got plenty of time. I just keep gently plodding on 'unhooking' and being myself. I am glad that I have tried to write about it, as it has triggered off thoughts which are really good.

Oddly enough during therapy I hardly discussed my relationship with my husband and yet now that I look at it I can see that the quality of the time he and I spend together has changed for the better out of all recognition. We have always thought we got on well – maybe it has something to do with the children all being mainly away now, but it's marvellous. I hadn't realised that he needed praise so much. We are much more spontaneous with each other now.

## Account 2: Mark

*Symptoms and feelings I had about them that led me to seek therapy*

The first symptoms I had were physical: bouts of giddiness, and tension in the head and neck muscles – it sometimes felt as though a clamp was being tightened around my head. In confined, artificially-lit buildings and crowded places, I began to have feelings of panic. My heart would pound and I would feel short of breath. I had this urgent need to run into the fresh air, or into an uncrowded space. I began to find difficulty in going out of the house – imagining all the bad events or feelings that I might experience. I became anxious and panicky before leaving home. 'Agoraphobia' the experts called it.

There were times when I thought I had a serious physical illness, but most often I simply thought I was going 'mad'. Night was the worst time. In bed my mind would dwell on fearful thoughts and feelings. First of all the tension would come, then the fear and anxiety.

I could find no-one amongst my friends or family in whom I could confide. They didn't seem to understand. 'Pull yourself together' was the commonplace and useless advice. I used to get a tight feeling in the pit of my stomach when I felt I was absolutely alone in the world. Confused and frightened I went to see the doctor. He diagnosed 'mild anxiety', prescribed a course of tranquillisers and arranged for me to see a psychiatrist at the 'out-patients' of the local General Hospital.

The inability of my family to support me seemed to emanate from two prejudices: that men did not suffer from 'problems with their nerves'; and that anybody who took tranquillisers was 'mentally ill'.

### Previous treatment and feelings about it

The plan was to visit a psychiatrist at a regular interval. My assumption was that he/she would establish the cause of the 'problem' and that my 'illness' could be cured. This was a simple and naive supposition that was quickly shattered by my subsequent experiences.

I saw several psychiatrists over the time I attended the out-patients clinic. I rarely saw the same one on consecutive visits.

With each new face I had to explain again my symptoms and feelings, and even recount my recollections of previous consultations. This did not happen, however, with one 'first-time' psychiatrist. He simply read my file notes and asked, 'Have you ever felt like picking up a knife and stabbing somebody?' This bolt out of the blue upset and offended me. I thought he had read something in my notes which others had failed to see, or worse, that the other psychiatrists were engaged in a conspiracy of silence while they got to the bottom of my 'problem'. This did nothing to alleviate the deep uncertainties I had about myself.

I only occasionally saw the psychiatrist to whom I had originally been assigned. On one visit he prescribed a drug called

'Nardil'. There was a card warning one of the dangers of eating or drinking certain listed products whilst taking the drug. One night after drinking $1/2$ pint of lager – permissable under the card regulations – I had a thunderous pounding begin in my heart; over the following 20 minutes, it gradually worked its way up into my head. I never felt so terrified in all my life; I was sure I was going to die!

At my next visit I explained to the psychiatrist what had happened. He decided that the mixture of Nardil, lager and 'bananas' (not on the list of 'don't eats'!) had reacted together and caused a potential stroke. He smilingly, almost triumphantly, proclaimed to a student psychiatrist present at the consultation, that this experience was 'something you won't come across very often', and with a disarming casualness, assured me that I had strong blood vessels!

When I did challenge the validity of the 'treatment' I was receiving at the out-patients' department, my assigned psychiatrist, a 'leading' figure in the local psychiatric community, squashed such temerity by becoming aggressive. In a raised voice (on one occasion he banged his fist on the table), he made veiled threats about treatments available for full-time patients at the local psychiatric hospital.

Over time I became totally demoralised. There seemed to be a bankruptcy of ideas about the 'cause' of my 'illness'. It began to seem as though 'mental illness' was as much a mystery to the psychiatrists as it was to me! The insensitivity, even indifference, of some of the psychiatrists was appalling. To be regarded as a specimen, to feel estranged from the psychiatrist who neither took you into his/her confidence, or gave you any credibility, left a void that could not be filled by trust. It was a void that grew larger as I lost faith in the profession and the system.

With the assistance of a letter from my GP – a source of constant support – one of the psychiatrists arranged for me to attend group sessions for agoraphobics at the local 'mental' hospital. The group consisted of patients, about ten of us, and was led by two psychologists. The group, prompted and guided by the psychologists, would talk about the feelings of anxiety and panic they experienced. The emphasis was very much on stressful situations and how that stress could be reduced. I was personally told not to add 'stress' to my life by reading and

writing (i.e. thinking!). As I write, I am in my final year of an
English Literature degree. The recommended 'solutions' to the
problems were improvement of 'social skills' and learning to
control feelings of anxiety and panic whilst in stressful situations.
For my own part I made no progress. I was still looking for
the cause of my anxieties, and I began to see that this was not
the way these psychologists looked at the problem. I was a
person living in the present, who for them had no past; and it
began to seem for me as though I had no future. About eighteen
months after I first went to see my GP, I felt no nearer to
discovering the sources of my anxieties. I felt I had wasted my
time. Frustrated and increasingly depressed I went back to
the GP who suggested I might have an interview with a
psychotherapist who had recently joined the practice. I felt
anybody was worth a try at this stage.

*My attitude and expectations about psychotherapy prior to
embarking upon it*

I attended my initial interview with a great deal of scepticism.
As I saw it the psychiatrists and psychologists I had seen thus
far (and they were legion) had failed dismally in understanding
me and my problems. There were, however, two brighter spots.
Firstly, my GP had recommended the psychotherapist, and he
was the only person left in whom I had any trust. Secondly, I
felt that my past was important to my present anxieties, and
nobody had yet engaged with me in looking at it in any depth. I
knew that if I searched long enough, somebody would. So it
was with feelings of doubt and reluctance that I entered upon
my first interview.

*My experience of psychotherapy*

The early sessions were characterised by my feelings of
discomfort and embarrassment. What I found, however, was a
person who was listening to what I was saying and seemed to
understand some of the pain I was experiencing. A feeling of
space began to emerge in the sessions; a sense that I was an
important person in the relationship, and that I had some control
both over the discussion and the pace of it. I was free to talk

about or not talk about anything under the sun. It meant that I began to trust someone, and in turn began to trust myself again.

The anxiety and panic were seen as manifestations of conflict within my life, and the therapy sessions gave me a pressure-free opportunity to roam these troubled waters of my life. The therapist focused my various meanderings and utterances onto three key areas: family life, work life, and sexual relationships. With suggestion, prompting and discussion, I began to understand more clearly the marital relations of my parents and my consequent family role. The emotional, sexual and power relations of the family group had repercussions upon my own sexual and social life which began to make sense of the way I felt and acted towards others, and also how others felt and acted towards me.

Fundamental was the view of my relationships to my mother and father. Unconsciously it was one of dependence and fear respectively. Crucially, when I attempted independence, paralysing panic struck at my mind affirming my helplessness, dependence and fear – a nasty and vicious circle. In the therapy I was able to realise this consciously and see that I had a false self-image and a false sense of me in the world. This 'truer' sense of myself worked to erode the panic and anxiety. The more I was thus able to effectively act and diminish the falsehood of my dependence and fear, the more the panic and anxiety diminished. It is the 'vicious circle' becoming a 'benign circle'.

Crucial then was the coming to consciousness of my 'false' and 'true' self. It is the *process of realisation* which is the most valuable aspect of the counselling experience of therapy. By talking about your feelings you can start to ponder the truths or falsehoods of your 'self'. Your experience in between sessions can affirm or deny these truths, as can a liberated memory, and also one's dreams.

Dreams were very important in prompting new understanding. In the sessions, we began to look at my dreams to see what they were saying about my state of mind. One dream I had during therapy was that of two policemen drinking at the bar of a pub. I came into the pub and handed one of them a bunch of flowers. This dream seemed to show a recognition of 'power' and 'emotion' as sources of conflict in my life. The dream symbolised a change in those relations within my life.

*Comments about changes*

Discovery and growth were the central experiences of therapy.
At first that growth was imperceptible, and I often despaired of
getting anywhere – yet at the same time I sensed I was in the
right place talking about the right things. Eventually I did begin
to experience development in my mental and emotional state.
The faster I began to grow the faster I grew. I was able to
reduce my intake of tranquillisers and panic states became less
regular and less severe. The clearer sense of my past and present
self helped me to understand or resolve mental and emotional
conflicts which in turn subverted feelings of anxiety, tension and
agoraphobia.

There were also corresponding changes in my practical and
material circumstances. One major change was in the work
sphere. Unsatisfied by my role as a Projects Engineer within
the tangled web of the industrial complex, I became a labourer.
Meanwhile I went to night classes and ended up where I am at this
moment, reading a degree in English Literature at University. I
also sorted out the negative feeling I had long harboured against
the Catholic Church, within which I was brought up. I recognised
that I had no fundamental identification with what the church
stood for, and so we parted company. Indeed more generally,
there have been profound changes in my personal, social and
political relations which have enhanced the quality of my life.

*Current position*

I still have uncertainties and doubts about myself, but the
movement from a position where life was becoming intolerable
to one where it offers a good deal of emotional and intellectual
satisfaction speaks volumes for the beneficial effect of
psychotherapy. Colouring that perception is the feeling of
belonging less to a people, a place and a way of life. Mostly
perhaps as a consequence of leaving the family and friends I
grew up with, but that I was only strong enough to do this
because of the therapy. Conversely I have learned the true
worth of friendship and family ties.

One piece of advice I would offer to anybody going for
psychotherapy is to believe and trust in yourself. Midst the fears

and doubts of your brittle psychological condition, listen to that remote voice whispering from within. It will tell you whether the treatment you are receiving is right for you. You will know when the therapist is or is not addressing your anxieties in a meaningful way. If you are unsatisfied with your treatment, then say so. If you get an inadequate response, seek advice and support elsewhere. Be persistent, no matter how hard it is, and you will find somebody who can give you the kind of support and help you need. Listen to that inner voice, at first a whisper, at last a shout. It pulled me through.

## Account 3: Hilary

*Description of symptoms and feelings about them that led to psychotherapy*

(a) Explosive diarrhoea, which sent me to the loo as often as three times an hour. Blood loss.
(b) Soreness around the rectum because of 'leakage'.
(c) Stomach cramps.
(d) Intestinal noises that were embarrassing.
(e) Total inability to control the rectum – and consequent distressing 'accidents' that led to a fear of going anywhere public, and especially to places where a loo would not be on hand.

To begin with (in the February/March when I didn't know what the matter was) I was simply frightened.

When I learnt that my mother had had similar symptoms with colitis, part of me accepted the condition as the 'family disease'. I was almost pleased with this proof that I was like my mother!

Later when the symptoms were worse/more frequent, I was angry with myself for my failure to get satisfaction from the hospital. I was annoyed that 'they' couldn't just give me a drug to cure the problem. I felt I was treated as an ignoramus; I disliked the doctor's patronising 'dear' as he spoke. I wanted a cure, yet I loathed going.

I also felt dirty and degraded by my symptoms: I resented that this condition interfered with my attempts to be efficient and well-groomed.

Later, when the therapy enabled me to understand why I had the symptoms, I saw them as annoying. My conscious mind could not control my body, and it was a long time before I accepted this fact.

### Previous treatment and my feelings about it

I had from the GP some 'Salazopyrin' tablets that acted as a mild 'disinfectant'. When I was losing blood, and the symptoms were at a 'high', I had some 'Colifoam' – a rectal foam which soothed the inflamed rectum with cortisone.

I took some time to discover what the action of Salazopyrin was – my enquiries led to evasions. Because I didn't understand it, I had little faith in it. After several bouts that were severe, I lost faith in the treatment altogether – except for the 'Colifoam', which I realised acted rather like a plaster on a sore finger – a temporary help whilst real healing is awaited.

I therefore realised that I had no real treatment of the cause – only of the symptoms.

### My attitude and expectations about psychotherapy

My expectations of psychotherapy were not raised at all, because of the precipitate arrangements between hospital and GP. On one Thursday, the hospital doctor recorded my view that my condition was caused by me. I thought that I would be channelled to someone who would teach me to relax, perhaps with a 'feedback' machine – or to someone who would help me *visualise* my condition and thereby to overcome it. Early the next week I had a telephone message from the GP asking me to call the therapist. I had no idea what to expect.

Consequently, I was unaware of any 'attitude' towards psychotherapy.

### The actual experience of psychotherapy

Of course, my feelings changed throughout the six months. To begin with, I was hostile because of scorn I had at that time for most things 'Freudian'. I was also rather belligerent because I felt some pressure was being put on me to conform as a female and produce children. Later sessions were never things of dread: I came to see my sessions as indulgences – I talked about myself all the time, and it was legitimate! I came to refer to the therapist to friends as 'my lady' (e.g. 'I can't come then – I shall be seeing my lady').

Yes, sessions were variable. I did feel cross with myself for crying (at first) and often felt painful emotion. Sometimes, I felt ridiculously naive for not having realised something. At other times, I felt victorious, even vindicated, when a view I had held in a 'battle' with my husband/parents was condoned (or deemed by me to be condoned). I often left feeling extremely hopeful that my relationships were now going to be just fine. I often left with ideas that I felt I wanted to discuss with my husband.

I was saddened to realise that the 'lift' experienced at the end of sessions did not last long, but this did not stop me from arriving in hope at the next session.

I did meet some surprises: I had not realised how insecure I was as a person until I came to see much of my behaviour as defence mechanisms. I have never stopped to think why it was that I insisted on behaving as an 'equal to men', and was shocked to realise it could stem from my relationship with my father. One 'surprise' that has been useful is coming to see my father as a victim: he had only previously been the perpetrator of misdeeds in my mind. As soon as I saw him mentally in the situation of having wrongs perpetrated on him too, I was able to understand why he'd behaved as he did – it was not malice to me!

I remember particularly one dream that I had recorded, in which my father was shut in a small railway hut, and I was sent to persuade him out. I was embarrassed to go as I was naked, and wearing a sanitary belt and towel . . . Another dream was of my cat removing her fur as though it were a sweater (her fur at the time of the dream was marred by a malodorous wound and bald patch) and playing under a car, tidying away her excrement by putting it under the wheels (presumably my obsession with cleanliness and tidiness).

Some of the most significant talk made it feel O.K. for me to go ahead with friendship with a woman – I'd not had a girlfriend for 20 years.

## Comments about changes that happened

I began to make efforts to talk with colleagues and more importantly to listen to them. This did bring about greater happiness during the day – as I was to believe it would. I saw that as I grew in the feeling of 'belonging', I did enjoy others' company. I understood the importance of 'making the effort'.

I did try to be less of a perfectionist. This I found hard – and I resented 'lowering my standards'. I found that I veered in the opposite direction – forcing myself to be 'sluttish', and then feeling annoyed that I'd been such a fool as to *force* myself to do anything, as that was what the problem was all about; imposing a mode of behaviour on myself.

I did not realise that I'd become analytical: I did often ask myself, 'Why are you doing this? In what role are you doing this?' I was gladdened by this: I saw it as a positive step.

Privately, much exploration went on. In later months, I spoke to no-one of the sessions: they were intensely 'mine'. I wanted to succeed in getting rid of my symptoms, and consequently wanted the sessions to be directed to that end only – I felt I was on the road to knowing myself.

## Current position

I stopped the sessions at the end of August, some six months after beginning. It seemed very long at the time of finishing, but now it seems a brief interlude.

I am more than glad for the sessions. Without the exploration made possible by therapy, the hypnosis for relaxation that followed could not have worked. I feel very privileged: something special happened during those six months that has made me adult – responsible for myself.

I would have no hesitation in advising someone to seek psychotherapy. My own good health and happiness have acted as an 'advert' already; my colleague has started a course of similar sessions.

## Gains

I do feel *feminine* now: I have truly 'killed' the idea of emulating males. I am happy with the 'different but equal' idea. I would quite like to be pregnant. I have a fuller life – I challenged myself to do something else but work! A more peaceful life – I do relax more and worry less!

## Losses

I feel a *little* nostalgia for my old motto, 'There is yet more in you', by which I used to drive myself, and make myself feel noble. My rule is now common sense – far more hum-drum!

## Effect on symptoms and feelings

I was frustrated that understanding in the conscious mind produced so few results in the subconscious. With hypnosis, I found a bridge between the two. Within five weeks of linking hypnosis to what I'd gained through therapy, my symptoms disappeared. The symptoms of a churning stomach and desire to rush to the loo reappeared during a 36-hour rather distressing voyage one Easter. On arrival, my 'self-hypnosis' relieved all tension, and the feelings went. I am now so tolerant of other adults – I can always find something to like, or some excuse for others' behaviour. This has made me rather more confident in my job, when I need to relate to others in the department.

## Account 4: Olga

There had been moments during my childhood when I felt detached from events and relationships. An unsettled, dizzy feeling would descend like an unexpected and unwanted visitor, and I would shiver in the summer heat of the desert city in which I lived. I experienced the presence of a thin, transparent wall, which set me off from my immediate surroundings. I knew it wasn't REALLY there, but I couldn't get through it or around it. I was carrying it with me. The strong, persistent heart beat that threatened to choke me, would rise up with the frustration of being sealed off from others. I later came to learn it was panic.

As a child, these moments were infrequent, but intense. For much of my adolescence, they rarely came. In the last few months of my 20th year, in my second year at College, however, the same sensations descended on me with no indication that they would depart. The unwanted 'visitor' came to stay. Terror moved in and claimed special attention. Under its influence, colours crowded my vision and popped around my head like fireworks. The shapes and sizes of buildings and trees moved and altered in a display designed to convince me I was crazy, and my heartbeat smashed against my throat like I had swallowed a perpetually beating bass drum. I needed some help. I was watching this happen while I was in the centre of it. Some untouched, but uncomfortable bit of me was still free enough to know that something could and needed to be done. I came home wailing. My parents 'phoned our family doctor and found me a psychiatrist.

Living in a culture which took seriously the issues of emotional health made it easier to seek psychiatric assistance. My parents and I were ill-equipped to find solutions just amongst ourselves. They, too, went to the therapist to get help in understanding my condition. Unable to eat, or sleep unassisted by drugs, I trailed after them like a toddler terrified of being left alone. Within a few months of therapy, it was just the doctor and me. They remained supportive in the background while I remained at the centre of my confusion and distress.

I entered therapy with few expectations. I was so uncomfortable with the physical symptoms that I looked upon my therapist as someone who would give me relief. 'Acute anxiety', he called it. He described my physical condition better than I could describe it myself. That helped. However, these were early days. I had no idea at the time that these symptoms were connected to real events and relationships, that my family biography wrote the parts which I was now playing. I learned this later on. As these first weeks went by, accumulating into months, the panic continued. Each day looked like the previous one; I awakened to seconds of calm but the bass drum would then resume its beating. Palpitations of the heart and shortness of breath were accompanied by icy hands and fuzzy vision. It began to occur to me that this was it – for the rest of my life.

Slowly we jointly explored my attitudes and my physical being. Part of me enjoyed the mental effort. My personality was being dismantled as long forgotten images and ideas were being rooted out and opened for observation. This must have done some good. I was still alive and engaged in my college studies. I was, nonetheless, still in a fog. My mind was cluttered with words that seemed unconnected with each other. What was happening to me seemed unattached to the world of my present being.

Whatever was wrong with me, the message seemed to say, had to do with me and me only. And, whatever that wrong was, it had to do with me – as a female. On the too few occasions when my therapist helped me to collect those scattered words and put them into thoughts, I was informed that my 'problem' was connected with an inability to commit myself to a man. I resented this; somehow I was able to form that opinion. But, I was terrified at resenting this, because that resentment was an expression of my 'illness'. Wasn't it? Anyway, how did he know this? Did he understand something which I didn't? Could he control me? Why didn't he let me in on my own secrets?

My visits were frequent and they enabled me to continue my studies. I remained in college, and gradually joined in the political movements growing up on campuses around the country. One of these was Women's Liberation. Reading and discussion with other women provided new ways of understanding that my personal agony was tied in some way to my political anger. I began to understand that circumstances outside of my mind had much to do with the bewilderment within it. Change those circumstances and perhaps I could change my life? I liked that idea. I just didn't know how to do it.

The end of my College course was approaching. I had to make a decision about my near future, and found that this was easier than anticipated. My college friends were going to continue with their studies and this suited me, as well. My options were pretty limited; post-graduate studies were expensive and my own university suggested I go elsewhere. I was living away from home, but leaving this college for another meant a new home in a different part of the country. I was up to it. I had to be.

My parents decided to separate and my mother moved out of town. The University near her accepted me, and my change of campus and abode were accomplished. I also had to change my

therapist. This was the real problem. I didn't like much of his
style or his approach, but it was all I knew. I was clearly stronger
than I had been when I began and there were now whole days
when the banging in my chest was calm and my hands would
warm to room temperature. I assumed that HE had 'fixed' some
bit of me. He had tinkered with my brain. What would
happen, I wondered, if some new therapist were a less qualified
'technician'. I didn't know at the time that it was me – with his
assistance – who was responsible for my improvement. That
discovery came later.

With my new round of studies began a series of adventures
in therapy. Recommendations from college friends took me
from one 'initial interview' session to another. It dawned on me
that I had opinions, now, about what suited me in a therapist.
To my pleasure I found myself acting on those opinions and
finding the emotional resources to reject some of the
arrangements which were on offer. In the midst of still painful
muddle, there emerged a confidence to make judgements about
such important things. My distress came with the belief that the
confidence was accidental, that it would leave as quickly as it
came. But then I also believed that my illness – as I still
understood it to be – was lurking on the edges of my sensibilities
and that it would come again unannounced to disable me. One
therapist suggested group work. That was fine for others, but
not for me.

He also charged interest on outstanding debts. These were
incurred if one's bill wasn't settled on the day of counselling.
He told me that paying interest was an incentive to emotional
well being. I was a student, with no financial assistance. Such
an arrangement as he suggested would have the opposite effect!
I walked out and never went back.

Another therapist was more liberal with his accounts. This, and
his well stocked food pantry, created a congenial environment in
which to talk. His style was considerably more structured than
that of my very first psychiatrist, but the themes were much the
same. There was something FUNDAMENTALLY WRONG
with me; that tinkering and tailoring my ideas would create the
'right' combination of thoughts and I would then settle in to
emotional stability. He was, however, the master tailor, and the
tinkering went on within me. The connection between me, my

emotional distress and the world of relationships and events outside of me was rarely discussed. There was, thus, no way I could understand the causes of my condition or the circumstances under which I would find health.

I didn't hold out much hope. That bit that was fundamentally wrong seemed to be bound up with my being female, and I reckoned it was more difficult to tamper with this. Even if I understood my sexual identity more clearly, I thought myself unable to change the way others behaved towards me. I suspected that much of this had to do with my relationship to the men in my family.

I had been the subject of abuse from an early age, and the pattern had been repeated. The fact of the abuse was not contended. The agent responsible, however, was in question. I believed that I had invited this attention and later, in therapy, I lacked the confidence to publicly investigate this version. I had been quite young, and members of my family had held both power and authority over me. 'Fitting in' to a society which makes being female 'a problem' presented me with puzzles that this therapist, like the others, couldn't solve.

My first year as a post-graduate finished with some successes. I had completed the coursework and had identified a topic for my thesis. Otherwise, I felt out of control. The physical symptoms of breathlessness, cold hands and rapid heart beats continued. The company of other students was unsatisfying, and there was no way to tell if that had to do with 'the illness' or a real difference of interests and background. When given the option to come to England on an academic exchange programme I knew this was for me. Despite pleas from my family to remain in America, I turned my efforts to the task of getting to England. It was then that I realised that I was fleeing from my family and I wondered whether just one ocean would be enough to keep them away. So many years in therapy and I had never explored my present relationship with my parents. Psychoanalysis had been entirely backward, and inward looking.

My studies in England went well. The change of environment had done important things for me and emotional health was being restored. I had benefited from my therapy, certainly, but as I began to take control over my life the gaps in my understanding were becoming easier to recognise. The mysteries of the events leading to 'my breakdown' hovered on the edges of my confidence and I still tumbled into troughs of despair, depression and anxiety. Another brief encounter with a psychologist provided me with some practical devices for dealing with stress. I needed more.

I was already attending a medical clinic where there were counselling provisions. I hesitated in arranging an interview. Preparing myself for yet another introduction to a new therapist was wearying. I was also feeling that there were different traditions in American therapy, and although they hadn't been as useful as I had hoped, they were what I knew. Some crisis at the time, however, threatened to undermine my studies and a new relationship I had formed. I couldn't afford to think about the therapy for much longer. I 'phoned in and an interview was booked.

The first session was easy. It was clear that the therapist and I spoke the same language. If my brain was to be tinkered with, at least this therapist had all the right tools. That was all I had hoped for, anyway. By now I had become accustomed to expect just enough of the right conversation to relieve the physical symptoms. To expect more never occurred to me. This time the therapist was a woman. She made it easy to talk about some of the sexual dimensions of my anxieties. On previous occasions I felt like I was the main attraction of a peep show. We agreed that I would return to continue with therapy.

The symptoms began to subside, but other things were happening as well. She firmly placed our initial discussions in the present. My well being was conditioned by my current relationships and activities and these needed as much serious attention as I had given the past. As therapy continued, the past was reintroduced. We jointly explored recurring themes and I began to make sense of a lifetime of methods – no longer appropriate – that I had devised for my psychic survival. I was addressed as an intelligent human being who got into trouble because of conflicting demands made by those whom I loved and needed.

There were present in these discussions important elements missing from the others. I was connected with my current surroundings. I was made to see that my 'illness' was a reasonable consequence of unreasonable demands by others and misunderstandings by me. The therapist was committed to a political understanding of sexual issues – individual paradoxes were conceived as political conflicts. For me, there had to be more for women than what is currently on offer. That's not a problem of my own making. Therapy became organized. Its objective was to restore choice to my life in circumstances where old patterns of surviving, pursued because they were familiar, were nonetheless inappropriate for my new needs and wishes. Those patterns were becoming available to me, as the therapist didn't claim special access to my secrets which only she could reveal. She wasn't a technician. I wasn't being 'fixed'.

The discomfort I once believed would be a permanent feature returns from time to time. I understand now that it is indicative of some pattern which current circumstances seem to reproduce. On most occasions I can identify the theme and the discomfort goes. It is clear I no longer have to settle with just getting by. I find myself increasingly at the centre of me. At first this was an occasional experience. Now it is the welcome visitor who seems likely to remain.

There is much I could say about my particular problems, but they are not important here. I think they work in much the same way for most people. Through therapy, we can work at gaining access to ourselves in ways which will restore choice and control in our lives.

## Account 5: Patricia – The experience of psychotherapy for psychosomatic vaginitis

I believe that psychotherapy gave me a 'new life'. This is *not* melodramatic, but true. And what's more, I felt a new person after only three sessions. It is living proof that psychotherapy is essential and ought to be incorporated into the normal Health Service, with psychotherapists working alongside GPs. It is because this situation does not exist that there is still a stigma attached to psychosomatic illnesses. Something very natural is not allowed to be seen as such, instead it verges on the taboo, and is certainly viewed by many as abnormal.

Because of this situation, I, for one, was not prepared to admit to myself for a long time, although I had an inkling subconsciously, that my very real, physically apparent illness, was psychologically induced. This recognition must be the first and most important step towards recovery. After all, it's *better* to be ill psychologically than physically once you *know* it's psychological because then you can control it and tell it to go away. It really works! The therapist gave me new hope and took a physical weight off my mind during my first talk with her. I'd had this black cloud which I could almost see for the two years of my illness; this symptom was, in fact, for me the most worrying of all. It was, as it were, 'concrete' depression and I *could not* clear my head of it. It tired me out, made me feel drawn and pale, and took away all the zest for life I'd had before. I was transformed from a really active, lively, self-confident person to someone who crawled around, was lethargic and passive.

Fortunately for me, although I made myself cry through self-criticism, and although the therapist suggested that this element of self-criticism probably helped to induce my psychosomatic vaginitis in the first place, it was this very self-criticism which also led me to persevere. It was the only active element left in me, and it drove me to carry on going to doctors – I must have seen about ten, plus a gynaecologist and dermatologist.

After going into hospital for a week with the strong faith that I'd be totally cured and, in fact, coming out worse, I was desperate. I was really depressed, but thought I was exaggerating and got cross with myself for being unhappy. I began to think I was a hypochondriac, and stopped talking about the vaginitis at all to anyone (I'd mentioned it to close friends after about a year, and it was such a relief to talk about it that I think I probably became a bit of a bore – although they assured me that I didn't when I asked them!)

I didn't mention it to my parents until much later, I was so intensely embarrassed – which was the worst thing possible because I now realise, talking about it was, in fact, a sort of brief catharsis, and keeping it all bottled up made it *intensely* painful. And when I say painful, I *mean* it; I felt as though I wanted to pull the inside of my vagina out – I can remember that feeling now. It got unendurable during my final exams.; I couldn't even sit down. I had to revise standing up! And of course I couldn't concentrate.

I kept on going to the doctors at London University, and they tended to be very rude to me, and I felt guilty about wasting their time. But they stuffed me with pessaries, cream, painkillers, etc. – which all had horrible side-effects. I felt permanently sick, had an awful headache and developed a thick brown vaginal discharge. My stomach became permanently distended – and, of course, my self-confidence went down even lower! Then when I went home it took a new turn. I developed a violent backache which, after a couple of weeks, spread into the ribs. It was so acute in the end that I couldn't even walk – and, what was worse, I couldn't lie in bed, I was so sensitive. It was agony the moment I bent my body or touched anything. Now I *really* thought I was a hypochondriac, and didn't say anything for a long, long time. But my parents noticed in the end – it was impossible to hide! They sent me off to the doctor, who checked my kidneys and sent me back saying there was nothing whatsoever the matter with me. It was after this that I saw a dermatologist privately and was sent into hospital.

When I came to Birmingham in October, to carry on with my studies, I felt really unhappy. But at a party I went to, I met a young man who became my boyfriend – my first boyfriend. I'd always been frightened of taking the step before, although I'd wanted to have a boyfriend . . . and now, for what was then an unknown reason, my pain would very often leave me briefly, especially when I was with him. But I lacked all self-confidence and could never enjoy myself properly in his company; I was always comparing myself with my former, other self. Nonetheless, it obviously boosted my ego quite a bit – but the crunch came. I didn't feel able to sleep with him, and after putting the question several times, he simply walked out on me. I was heart-broken, and my vaginitis got ten times worse.

It was at this point that my GP sent me to a therapist – thank goodness! For the first time, I felt that here was a person who really understood. She gave me a series of accounts written by women who had been through the research study into psychosomatic vaginitis. They described how they had felt and how their condition had improved. I read them the night I got them after a really depressed, painful day. In five minutes the fog in my head had lifted and the pain in my vagina had disappeared. It came back intermittently during the next few days, but I was so happy, I already felt a new person. It didn't get me down unduly even when it did come back, because I knew that I could make it go away again.

Soon I had another, and really special, boyfriend, and what with a gigantic boost of the ego and further talks with the therapist, I became 90 per cent better. I've still got to conquer the other 10 per cent – and in times of emotional upsets, it becomes something like 20 per cent – but I firmly believe that I can do it. I've recognised that my illness was induced both by a fear of men and of expressing my sexual feelings. I've got rid of this fear now and am healthy and full of confidence. I enjoy life again and even look, as well as feel a different person. It's great – and all because of a bit of psychotherapy!

# 8   The Use of Therapy

## A process for change

Although the accounts by the five people in the previous chapter of their experience of therapy are very different, they have one factor in common. Each client showed that it was the understanding that they gained of themselves through therapy that played an important part in enabling them to change their lives.

When Margaret (Account 1) began therapy she was so caught up with the 'bad fairy' vision of herself that she had become exhausted by striving to be the 'good fairy' to counteract it. For Mark (Account 2) his dependence on his mother had left him feeling so involved with her that he was unable to separate from her enough to get a secure sense of himself. This was particularly so after his father died. His level of anxiety was almost unbearable and he felt that he had a great deal of appeasing to do. In particular, this was experienced in relation to father figures, shown so clearly in his dream of offering flowers to the policemen.

Hilary (Account 3) had conflict centred around her sex, as she had to overcome feelings that to be female was equated with being second rate. Olga (Account 4) also felt 'bad' about herself, perceiving herself as 'wrong' because she was female. In some way she felt this must be the cause of the abuse she had experienced. She could not change her 'femaleness'. This conflict had led to a sense of confusion, and at times severe panic. Patricia (Account 5) discovered very quickly that she could discard her very painful symptoms, as she did not need them to protect herself from expressing her sexuality.

These accounts illustrate in their different ways the major use or purpose of psychotherapy. It offers people the opportunity to work for a greater understanding of themselves, which leads to change and growth in a way that *they* determine. It is not the therapist producing a 'cure' for a particular symptom with the client passively 'made better'. Psychotherapy is a hard struggle during which the clients use the unique relationship with the therapist, in order to explore the sources of the clients' conflicts and to help them to discover new and better ways of resolving them.

As some of the sources of the inner conflicts are recognised (for example feeling driven to 'hide' in some way because of not being valued in the eyes of one's parents) it becomes apparent that the sources of our inner conflicts are linked with the sources of conflict in society.

I believe that this is because these conflicts arise from deeply entrenched value judgements that stem from certain groups of people holding the power to determine the lives of others. (For example, adults over children, and in a patriarchal society, males over females, as described in Chapter 2.)

It is for this reason that therapy is perceived as a political activity. It can be used to uphold and enforce traditional value judgements. It can also hold the possibility and, I believe, does hold the responsibility to challenge some of our society's current values. This is particularly so in the area of valuing different people.

Therapy does challenge such value judgements in a minor way, by giving great importance to the feelings of individuals. People have an increased sense of worth when their deepest concerns are listened to with care. For many people it is immensely validating to have another person's full attention focused on them regularly for an hour at a time. Ironically, this is particularly difficult for some women to accept. It is such a rare experience for many of them to be given this level of caring, that they sometimes find it quite hard to sustain.

When therapy is used by individuals in a constructive way, it enables them to 'unblock' their energies from unworkable 'neurotic solutions' and to apply them instead to ways of living that they experience as more fulfilling. As already suggested, the work required to examine the 'false perceptions' people hold about themselves which make up the 'blocks' is immensely complicated, time-consuming and at times deeply distressing.

## Recognising the sources of conflict

It is because of the unique way that the therapist and client work together that this task can be undertaken. When the relationship is built on trust (which in itself can take a long time to build) many people feel able to reach greater levels of openness and honesty about themselves than they have been able to achieve with life-long partners or friends. When people start to examine themselves in this way, they bring previously hidden aspects of their mind right up into their current awareness. These take the form of buried memories, and very often extremely fearful feelings. Sometimes they also experience amazing 'revelations'. I have heard many clients ask at such moments 'Why didn't I know that before? as they suddenly see with startling clarity a connection between a past experience and how they feel about themselves in the present.

For clients to be able to work in this way it is not only of utmost importance that they can trust their therapist, but equally important that *all* the client's feelings and thoughts are accepted by the therapist 'without prejudice'. What that means in practice is that the client feels fully heard, without condemnation or rejection, nor with any unspoken demands for appeasement or seduction. If the focus of the therapy is on striving to understand the client's feelings as these are expressed and shared with the therapist, then how and when they began, as well as their current forms, can be gently explored. In this atmosphere of trust, acceptance and careful exploration, clients can dare to express the deep pain, sadness, anger and feelings of hate. They can express their long-felt desires to be *different* from how they currently perceive themselves to be. As a result of this they no longer have to act out all their crushing experiences from the past.

The *compulsive* nature of the *need to repeat* our earlier experiences is one of the realisations that everyone in therapy is virtually forced to recognise.

The 'power' that has been used in a variety of forms, that has been experienced so oppressively in early childhood, when there was no means to escape, is now reapplied over and over again by the adult. This time round we do it to ourselves. Each time this occurs, energy goes into the old pattern of feeling 'stupid', 'bad', 'hopeless', 'ugly' or whatever the oppressed sensation may be and the person reaffirms their own sense of lack of 'power' to change it. One of therapy's primary tasks is to enable people, through understanding these patterns of behaviour and feelings, slowly to pull back the 'power' into themselves to change these negative perceptions. Above all therapy encourages people to determine more realistic views of themselves so that they can begin to shift the old feelings of being terrified, cowed or constantly angry.

One of the complications of therapy is that clients often resist the therapist's acceptance of them. Clients understandably distrust it and sometimes do their best to test it by trying to make the therapist reject them. Occasionally clients display the most extreme negative parts of themselves to test their 'acceptability' by the therapist. If these behaviours or attitudes are seen merely in terms of 'manipulation', and the client is trying to 'control' the therapist, a huge and invaluable opportunity for both client and therapist to perceive what is really going on is sadly missed. The therapy is likely to end abruptly with the client withdrawing and confirming once again their old beliefs felt from childhood that they are 'bad' and 'unworthy'. Paradoxically such a client can also feel a whiff of triumph as he or she resorts more firmly than ever, to their old 'neurotic solution', whatever it may be, and remain convinced it cannot be changed. This is because whatever was available in therapy was not perceived as strong enough, or perhaps continuing for long enough to enable the client to let go of the 'old patterns' and to try out alternative ways of being.

## Letting go of false perceptions

During therapy, clients come to discover just how *false* some of the perceptions that they hold about themselves are. They also come to recognise that it is these perceptions that so often provide the conflicting feelings that cause so much of their distress. Here follows a general and fairly common example.

Certain people behave in a very aggressive, critical, attacking manner with others, as if they were constantly expecting to be attacked themselves. Such people's earliest experiences have led them to protect themselves in this way. Originally, such a method of defence may well have been experienced as essential for their survival, but in their adult life its inappropriateness is very evident. Those around such a person in their family or at work respond either by becoming cowed and frightened (as the person once felt themselves to be) or they retaliate with even greater aggression.

This enables such a person to maintain their belief that the world is full of people who would 'do them down'. It also keeps hidden from them any recognition that it is *their* behaviour which plays such a big part in creating the aggressive response in others, and that this could actually be changed.

In therapy it is possible for such a person to begin to recognise that it is no longer necessary to confront every situation as if they were 'fighting to the death' for their space! With the therapist's caring support such a person is enabled to muster the courage to lay down the 'swords' he or she has carried since early childhood. Such a person then discovers that not only are the 'swords' not needed, but that people actually respond, often with patience and kindness when no 'swords' are around. This new and sometimes unbelievable experience enables the person to begin to believe in their own goodness.

As already described in previous chapters, such a 'new way' of being is at first strenuously opposed by all manner of 'sabotaging'. It challenges all that the person has believed in, generally as far back as he or she can remember. The 'good' feelings of being 'without swords' is such that, in spite of the sabotage, the person seeks them again. Gradually 'swords' are replaced with more appropriate behaviour that brings back such different responses that the person discovers that they no longer need to guard themselves by being permanently on the attack. The person's energies are then freed to work with other people, instead of defensively against them.

## Recognising the force of the 'sabotage'

Within the safety of therapy, when we can feel we will not be condemned as stupid, we are able to recognise how strongly we 'sabotage' our goals of being 'loved', 'successful' or 'seeking approval' in some way. Without the security of the therapeutic relationship I believe few people can manage to do this. One of the methods of 'sabotage' most commonly used is to deny the good things in ourselves and, without being fully aware of it, to avoid situations where they may actually be achieved. There is a further and much more complicated form of 'sabotage' that is generally fairly obvious to other people, but usually deeply hidden from the person concerned. This occurs when someone appears to be (and they strongly believe that they are) striving hard towards a goal that they want. In reality they have set the goal up in such a way that they cannot possibly reach it, and so it is doomed to fail. A man who greatly feared any close relationship (although he wanted one very much) thought he could deal with this fear by getting married. A swift courtship was followed by a wedding, but two days later he ran away from his wife. This is a perfect example of someone taking far too big a stride towards a goal which aroused an unmanageable amount of fear in him. He then felt compelled to turn away from it. Rather than have his wife in a position where he felt that she could abandon him (and so repeat his earliest experience with his mother) he gave his wife the pain he so feared having himself. He succeeded yet again in 'proving' to himself that a close relationship was 'dangerous' and not a possibility for him.

Such people who have felt under-valued by their parents and other adults for whatever reason during their childhood and adolescence, are frequently left with a deep sense of emptiness inside themselves. This feeling leads to a severe sense of conflict. On the one hand there is a strong seeking for love and approval from others to confirm a sense of their own value. In strong opposition to this, representing the 'other side' of the conflict, there is a strong rejection of the love that they seek. This is because receiving love and approval, although wanted so much, makes such a person feel helpless as they experience the sense of power this gives to another who could then withdraw their love. This sense of helplessness reproduces the experience of early childhood when love, needed so crucially, was unreliable or absent.

Unfortunately, some people strive for many years to get love and approval from parents who are incapable of giving it, believing that this is the *only* source from which to get their good feelings. A woman described banging at 2 am on the door of her elderly father's bedroom. She had always experienced him as deeply rejecting of her. She was shouting and demanding that he give her the love she felt that he 'owed' her. Later describing how she felt at the time, she said that 'it feels like a great thirst for something I must have; like water in a desert'.

In order to maintain this compulsive striving after love from one particular source, which may be parents or may be transferred to someone else, the possibility of obtaining it elsewhere has equally to be denied. Other people's love and approval is rejected or under-valued. Any form of approving of the self, or even seeking pleasure from other activities, tends to be rendered either impossible to find or perceived as worthless. In this way, such people maintain their own sense of helplessness and low value, as they fail to get the love and approval they need. They continue to believe that validation and love must come from one particular source, and fail to recognise that this way of feeling and behaving actually prevents them from finding it.

## Learning to find love

The solution to this conflict comes during therapy, when people slowly recognise *why* they feel so 'bad' about themselves. They gradually cease to demand love and approval from sources that will either never provide it, or not sufficiently, and recognise that this way of seeking only perpetuates their sense of helplessness. As each small step is taken away from the 'hopeless' source, and towards other sources such as new work, friends, creative activities or sports, so the person builds up a more realistic view of their own abilities and likeableness. Out of this comes the possibility of a new and rewarding close relationship, for there is no longer a demand to be completely valued and validated by another. The person is *doing some of it for themselves*. This new appreciation of themselves then becomes available for use in forming an equal and supportive relationship with another person, in which both can grow and develop.

Unfortunately for some people, if the pattern has been set up so that the 'wanting' love and approval led inevitably in the past to having 'nothing', so this expectation continues strongly into adult life. Safety is then perceived as lying only in making no move towards having anything! To 'seek' means only to 'lose' in such a person's experience, and this deep fear of further loss produces a sense of intolerable helplessness. Such people tend to spend a great deal of their lives withdrawn and on their own. They often feel intense loneliness, mixed with a sense of deep envy of others who appear to relate easily. The power which such people feel is held over them by others to recreate these experiences of intolerable deprivation, is exactly as it was originally felt in their early childhood.

## Facing feelings of loss

The safety of the therapeutic relationship enables us not only to look at how we 'sabotage' our own deepest wishes for love and approval, but also provides a place in which we can express our feelings about being deprived of love and the deep sense of loss this leaves us with. Whenever any of us block our wishes or turn away from the things that we want, we believe that we have controlled the loss for ourselves. In this way, we feel as if a 'worse loss' has been prevented. The 'worse loss', to be avoided at all costs, is always perceived as the intolerable sense of helplessness that comes from feeling that one is being controlled by someone else, or by some greater forces outside ourselves. When we are caught up in these losses it can feel as if we have no ability to control our lives at all.

Here are two further examples. Hazel lost two of her babies. One died due to a cot death and one to prematurity. She was experiencing feelings of extreme panic and could not face taking her youngest child to hospital, where she had had many of her traumatic experiences. She felt fearful of going out and was unable to travel or contemplate a holiday. Even local shopping had become extremely difficult. As she talked she recognised that although her feelings of terror had arisen as a result of her experiences, these feelings were also acting as a 'protection'. They were keeping her away from situations that might include more risk of loss, which at that stage she felt quite unable to cope with. Previously she had been someone who had always 'coped'. She was always the 'strong one' who had felt she must make everything right for everybody else.

When Gina discovered that her boyfriend still loved her after a temporary separation, she felt very happy and excited. Very rapidly, however, she started to feel that the relationship 'couldn't last'. Deep down she did not believe she could have a loving relationship. She was already preparing herself for the loss of it. As she began to feel downcast and low, in anticipation of it ending, so her boyfriend sensed her sad withdrawal from him. He too began to feel unsure. Her fear of a 'loss' that might come in the future, actually led to her creating the loss in the present.

During therapy, the sadness and pain experienced as a result of these feelings of loss need to be expressed, shared with and validated by the therapist, so that the client can move on. In this way the fear of repeating the old loss feelings are no longer used to 'block' the taking of risks that is inevitably involved when we move towards making new relationships or to try out new ways of working or behaving.

## The importance of fantasy in therapy

As therapy provides an opportunity to explore our deepest wishes and our worst fears, so it inevitably includes the world of fantasy. Exploring fantasy is a very important part of therapy. The client's fantasies will be the focus of attention, but therapists are also likely to be aware of some of their own.

Art and music therapy, and to a large extent psycho-drama, use the exploration of fantasy as their main therapeutic method. All these therapies offer people a way of experimenting with images. These may be drawn, painted, created in clay or perhaps danced to or acted out in some way. When we produce images or ideas in this way they always portray some inner perceptions we hold of ourselves, as well as how we see ourselves in our environment. Some understanding of these comes about as the therapist or other participators ask questions or make comments. It also comes as the person *actually experiences* re-living or expressing the feelings involved as they paint a picture or create a dance or music. This understanding can come in a particularly acute form at times in psycho-drama, when someone is encouraged to play the role of a person who plays an important part in their real life. To suddenly 'be' one's mother or partner and to say their words can lead to a new awareness of someone else's feelings.

## The use of dreams

Dreams are especially valuable in therapy because they are so intensely personal and usually highly significant for the individual.

They often show with startling clarity, even when in disguised form, exactly how we are feeling about our situation. This is particularly so when they show feelings of which we have previously been unaware or even want strenuously to deny. Sometimes they throw light on what we perceive the 'blocks' to be, through the symbols in the dream. Robert, (who felt driven to act out the fantasy 'charade' with his mother; see Chapter 3), had a dream of setting sail in a beautiful boat which he then realised was tethered to the bank. This dream could not have been more explicit in showing both how he experienced his separation anxieties to such a debilitating degree, and also perhaps the fruitless nature of sexual fantasies about his mother, which lay at the heart of his depression.

Many fantasies occur to us all when we are wide awake. These daydreams or building of images often have a consecutive aspect, like stories following each other. A woman shared her experience of deep anger and destructive feelings, expressed through the image of taking an axe to a large tree and felling it. This led on to a further image of hurling the axe up into a tree, but this time it only brought down a few branches. The image that followed this felt very different, as the axe changed and became golden. As she fantasised throwing this new rather beautiful axe into the tree, golden sparks descended from it. These images occurred when this woman had started a relationship which stirred deep loving feelings within her. These had in turn aroused some negative feelings about herself, that came from the rejection by her parents that she had experienced all her life. Through these fantasies the wish is expressed to transform the destructive angry feelings into positive ones as the 'gold sparks shower down'. When these sorts of fantasies are expressed it does not mean that the negative feelings will not recur. The person has become aware of them and is working on feelings to do with understanding and changing them.

I believe that it is very important to help clients move towards their own interpretations and understanding of their dreams and pictures, through gentle questions. This is far more likely to lead to their using this understanding, rather than when therapists impose some seemingly clever explanation of their own.

Freud was one of the early psychoanalysts to point out the value of dreams in therapy (1932). It is a vast and complicated subject and one to which a number of other analysts have also devoted entire books.

## The use of short therapy

Although the uses of therapy described in this book apply mostly to long-term therapy, which enables people to make changes in their life-long patterns of feeling and behaviour, short-term therapy has many very valuable uses as well. Patricia's description (Chapter 7, Account 5) of the changes that she experienced in her life show this very clearly.

Short-term therapy is generally understood to last a few weeks or months and it usually, though not always, works at a fairly superficial level. This does not mean that it is insignificant to the client. Such therapy is generally focused on to a specific concern or problem that the person wishes to make a decision about or attempt to change. This may concern their marriage, their children, or perhaps a move to a new field of work. It may play a vital part in supporting someone over a critical period of their life, such as a time when they are going through a divorce or bereavement following the death of someone very important to them.

I believe short therapy is more likely to be effective for someone who generally feels good about themselves, and has a perception of their 'normal way of being' that they strongly want to regain. This applied to Patricia, for example, who worked on understanding the cause of her severe vaginitis and was then able to resolve her conflicting feelings remarkably fast.

Occasionally the understanding of themselves that a person gains during a short period of therapy enables them to see their life-long pattern of beliefs and behaviour in a new light. The experience of resolving a conflict in one part of their life may then give them sufficient confidence to make similar changes in other parts. I believe this to be relatively rare, but when it does happen timing is of the utmost importance. It probably only happens when the person was right on the point of both wanting and feeling able to become aware of themselves at a deeper level.

## The limitations of therapy

It is a tragic fact that some people have experienced such terrible losses, such repeated deprivation, such cruel treatment from people who should have provided them with loving care, that they may be unable to use a therapeutic relationship to rebuild a new validation of themselves. Unfortunately, some people's actual experiences would be disbelieved or seen as sensationalist if written about in a book such as this.

It is most important that therapists do not unwittingly repeat an experience of severe loss or sense of 'let down' for their clients, by giving them another experience similar to the one that has been at the heart of their conflict. One of the reasons why psychotherapy is so often unsatisfactory in psychiatric hospitals, particularly in out-patient departments, is because of the rapid turnover of junior hospital doctors. It is not uncommon for someone to attend a hospital expecting to see the doctor they saw on their last visit, only to be informed that the doctor has left and a new one is in their post. Such experiences make it much harder for people to seek therapy again. Some therapists inadvertently give clients the old experiences of being controlled or devalued, which so many have already suffered from in the past.

## Therapists' needs

Therapists need good reliable support and supervision, if they are to remain in touch with their own vulnerability and yet feel able to work with people who may be in great distress. Unfortunately, good supervision for therapists is hard to find outside London, most of it has to be sought privately and it tends to be expensive. I believe that one of the great needs at present in this country is the provision of places where psychotherapy can be available within the NHS, in establishments which are not run as hospitals and where the client may reside for short or long periods.

Comparatively little psychotherapy is available through the NHS at present, but the demand for it is steadily increasing as people become more knowledgeable about the causes of emotional distress and mental illness. People are also now less willing to accept pills as their only treatment for severe anxiety or depression. The growth of therapy centres, some specifically for women, providing for the self-referral of clients to trained therapists who are not medical, is a new pattern of development. It would increase much more quickly if there were more training available, as well as funding from Health Authorities responsive to the demand for preventive mental health services.

**When seeking therapy**

Whatever type of therapy one seeks, it is important for people who are trying to find a therapist that they safeguard themselves as fully as they can, by requesting information both about the therapist's training and their supervision. This applies particularly to therapists who work privately or independently outside any recognised institutions. All therapists should be willing to provide this without being defensive. There is a useful section in Ernst and Goodison's book *In Our Own Hands*, which gives guidelines for people seeking therapy (1986). The type of questions clients can reasonably ask before they begin therapy are listed in detail.

# 9 Human Goals

## Learning to value the self

Whatever goals individuals *appear* to seek for themselves in life, there seems to be an imperative need for all of us to feel valued for ourselves. There are very many different ways in which people seek this valuation. Some seek it through making money, both because of the power that it brings and the possessions that they can buy. Others seek it through achievements in a particular field where their efforts bring recognition or applause. Many people seek it through a close relationship. Many women, particularly in the older age groups, base their valuation almost entirely on being needed by their family and friends.

It seems as if these apparent 'goals' are really only a means to a common end. This is the universal goal so deeply sought, of having a sense of 'self' that is both authentic and fully valued. Freud defined this in terms of the mature adult male with not only a strong 'ego', but also a high level of morality with a positive 'super-ego'. Many people today totally reject his argument that females are defined as those people 'without a penis'. They are categorised by gender as 'lesser beings', missing something so vital that this perception renders them physically, intellectually and morally inferior to males. The writings of such eminent psychoanalysts as Adler, Horney, Thompson and Moulton refute such a perception as false (see Baker Miller, 1973). In spite of this the idea of adult male superiority expressed in the phrase 'penis envy' still affects many psychoanalysts' way of thinking.

I believe that the deeply damaging effect of such a perception is to uphold the idea that differences between people must inevitably be seen in hierarchical terms. That is to say, that differences must have a value judgement: male to female and white to black. This huge struggle for superiority and domination profoundly affects the goals we seek and, above all, the positive sense of 'self' that as individuals we strive to achieve. As we examine how this positive sense of self is sought after, we see the contribution psychotherapy can make in increasing our understanding, both of the sources of a good evaluation and the many complicated 'blocks' to its achievement.

This sense of a valued self that feels real to us is not a static position. It is not a place that we reach and sit on like a plateau. It is a process of growth which we all seek to move towards and increase. Eric Fromm, in his book *To Have or To Be* (1978), describes in a very clear way his view of how people can strive towards it.

I believe that this positive, authentic sense of a fully valued self lies at the core of a good mental health. Dr Bowlby defines it as coming from 'good attachments' (1980), and Dr Baker Miller writes of it being developed 'through relationships' (1984). This concept of our sense of self being built through relating throughout our lives offers a very profound and important understanding of how we operate as human beings. Our very earliest patterns of relating continue to affect how we all relate as adults, both to our own children and to other adults.

Many people have experiences in their life that crush this sense of being a valued and authentic person. Contrary to general belief, such people do not necessarily come from families where there have been traumatic events, cruelty, neglect or even lack of affection. These patterns are set up because children feel compelled to behave in certain ways in response to demands put on them by parents, other relatives or other important adults. The commonest example of this is the way some people feel compelled to appease others all the time. They must never oppose, for to do so is felt to carry too big a risk of rejection. For these people appeasing appears to be their only way of operating, yet the price they pay is always some loss of their sense of authentic self. For others the very opposite patterning occurs. They feel driven into a rebellious way of being. Such people often describe themselves as feeling constantly angry. Whenever anyone in authority, or within an establishment in which such a person works, suggests how they should behave, this is always experienced as crushing and oppressive. However great a loss it is for the person concerned at a subjective level, they will oppose the rules, or the organisation, or whoever it is that brings back those early feelings of having to 'fight to survive'.

Some people oscillate between the two responses. They feel compulsively driven to appease, and then have such a deep sense of loss of self that they are quickly driven to rebel. The unpleasant and frightening feeling for such people is that they do not have a sense of 'being themselves'. They feel as if there is 'no room' for their real selves to operate in. They no longer trust their own feelings. They constantly expect to fail and to be rejected.

Therapists are in a unique position to hear how people continue to put these early patterns into effect over and over again. People who feel themselves to be 'bad' in whatever way, stick like glue to their 'bad' visions of themselves and 'sabotage' the good ones.

The sense of pain that people feel as they describe their sense of self as 'at the bottom' or always 'second best', is endlessly repeated as they often recreate the old dreaded feelings for themselves. A lovely invitation may be turned down or the opportunity of a new job is rejected; they are not perceived as possible to accept or believe in. Someone described how she hated the insecurity she felt being so short of money when unemployed. Later she realised, when earning a good wage, that she felt guilty every time she bought anything for herself. She was daring to oppose the old pattern of her 'worthless self' and finding it extremely hard to do so. Another woman described the difficulty of really enjoying her home. She had it furnished in ways that she hated and felt helpless to alter it.

For some people this pushing away of good, successful feelings seems to come because they are so patterned into bad unworthy feelings that they cannot feel deserving enough to claim any good ones. For others it feels that to have anything positive (love, achievements or success in any form) is perceived as so threatening to others that it is 'too dangerous' to claim, and that it will only bring hostility. This fear has of course a real aspect. Whenever women move to claim a space in areas of life previously dominated by men, they experience extreme hostility. This is as true for women who seek ordination in certain churches today, as it was many years ago when women struggled to become doctors.

This sense of helplessness to get what we want for ourselves is experienced by all humans when they are babies. It is no doubt the most persistent and potentially painful patterning for us all.

## The earliest experience of helplessness

Our very earliest 'good' feelings come from being lovingly cuddled, well fed, warm and comfortable; but these needs can only be met by the adults who care for us. When they are not met, we experience the greatest sense of total helplessness – our very survival is at stake. As we lie, able only to cry because we are hungry, cold, wet and lonely, we remain unable to supply any of these things for ourselves. So it is that we build up recognition that 'good' feelings come when our needs are met by some 'object' or 'person' 'out there'. 'Bad' feelings come when our needs are not met. For most of us the ability to cope with these 'bad' feelings that come from feeling deprived, empty, cold and lonely, comes from discovering that the 'good' is there in greater measure than the 'bad'. From this experience, as we grow through childhood and adolescence, we come gradually to feel ourselves sufficiently loved and of value. Throughout our childhood we have also to learn gradually about the strange and inconsistent ways of the adult world. We struggle to gain some measure of understanding in order to get our needs met. In this way our feelings of total helplessness get modified, as we learn how to please, to placate, to wait, to share and hopefully to get enough 'good' feelings about ourselves. If we are fortunate enough, the 'good' feelings are stronger than the 'bad', so that we learn to tolerate some levels of frustration and deprivation.

If the adults to whom we are attached as babies and young children give us messages that we are not wanted, or handle us so inconsistently that we never know whether our needs for love and nurturing will be met or not, or such adults change frequently or abandon us, and we become convinced we are not loved or valued, then the perception of our own 'goodness' becomes deeply threatened. Some children suffer very severe levels of rejection which lead to extreme feelings of helplessness and a deep sense of worthlessness. These beliefs are then taken on into adult life and continue to determine the negative way in which such people relate to others. For all of us this 'vision of ourselves', provided in childhood and adolescence by the adults who care for us, forms the basis of our own belief in being lovable. Above all it determines our perception about the love and approval that is available to us in the world outside as we grow up. One of the best known examples of this is Marilyn Monroe. Although she had riches, fame, beauty and talent, these worked so paradoxically as to increase her belief that no-one could ever love her for herself.

John Bowlby's studies describe clearly how we *continue* to wish for safe, loving, reliable attachments that will give us a belief in our own goodness, all our lives. It is this which he believes enables us to be effective and consistent people. Bowlby considers that this need for an attachment is not limited to early childhood, and that it should not be perceived as a 'babyish dependence' to be 'outgrown'. He sees it as the basis of strength which creates the confidence in which adults can operate effectively. He aptly describes this as the ability to act 'separately' and to 'explore'; that is to have the motivation to carry out the things we want to do. He sees both these abilities as springing from a good view of the self formed in turn from secure, reliable, loving attachments.

If we fail to obtain the love and approval that we need in early life, to give us a *good enough* view of ourselves with which to operate effectively, then we tend, whatever attachments are available in later life, to block or in some way 'sabotage' them. We do the *rejecting of them* in some form or another, rather than expose ourselves to the risk of relying on them and facing their subsequent possible loss, exposing us again to the sense of intolerable helplessness.

This process often occurs without the person being fully aware of it. They may realise that their relationships seem to be either shallow or shortlived – or they may describe themselves as 'always unlucky'. Their relationships, and also the ways they seek other goals too, nearly always follow a specific pattern with frequent changes. Often the closer or more important the relationship or goal becomes, the more strongly such people feel driven to reject them. It is understanding and working through such conflicts that is the stuff of therapy.

### The sources of conflict in society

On a different scale there are the objective forces in society that also operate most powerfully in affecting the views we hold of ourselves. These in turn affect the way parents treat children. One of the aspects of these forces that contribute to their power is that they also tend to be self-perpetuating. As male children tend to be valued more highly than females, so girls identify more closely with boys than boys feel able to do with girls. The same applies to white children and black ones. When a film was made recently to help children understand about hospital procedures with a view to helping them to overcome fear about operations, the child chosen to act in this was a white boy. Although it was important to choose a child that other children could identify with, the choice itself only helps to perpetuate the superior value given to a child who is male and white.

In our patriarchal society, boys who carry on the family name and inheritance are generally valued much more than girls. Many mothers only feel themselves fully valued if they can produce a son. There are of course individual situations that may be totally different from this generalised pattern when, for example, a number of boy children are followed by a specially treasured daughter. A first son may feel very pushed out by the arrival of subsequent twin sisters; but these individual variations are exceptions to the overall scene. Research has shown that boy babies tend to receive more nurturing than little girls (see Belotti, 1973) and more attention at school (see Spender, 1982). These perceptions become built into the girls' view of themselves, with low expectations continuing through their lives.

Because in general boys are given a far stronger message about their greater value, this enables boys to retain it for themselves more easily. This greater value given to boys through education and work opportunities tends to make them more effective in comparison to girls, in both 'separating' and 'exploring' the world outside.

Boys are discouraged very strongly from being emotional, because showing their feelings is perceived as 'weak'. The most frequent adult exhortation to young boys is 'not to cry' and to be 'big and strong'. In contrast, girls are encouraged to express feelings, and to know about them, but largely in order to offer emotional nurturing to others. Even today's girls are persuaded strongly to be docile and submissive in ways that boys are not. Recent research has shown that in mixed schools in particular, girls will sometimes hold back and choose not to compete with boys for fear of being rejected as 'not feminine', and their 'cleverness' being perceived as threatening to boys (see Stanworth, 1983).

This insidious pressure placed on girls to give more nurturing and care, and yet receiving less of it for themselves, combined with feelings that they must deny their own abilities for fear they will be spurned by boys, makes it much harder for girls to feel good about themselves, and to retain a strong sense of self-direction.

Many women also find it hard to achieve good feelings about themselves, except in the terms prescribed for them through serving other people. This does not make serving others in itself a 'bad' thing, but such work tends to be grossly under-valued because it is generally provided by women. Many women live their lives enabling men to perform theirs – either as daughters, girlfriends, wives and mothers. As Jean Baker Miller (1976) pointed out, if women attempt to get a more even sharing of these nurturing tasks they are often charged with being 'selfish' or 'greedy'. Women may also feel some sense of hopelessness when this serving of others is experienced as the only source of worth for themselves that they know. It can also hold a deep resentment, because it is under-valued and leads to a sense of being 'second rate'.

The pressure on boys to be 'brave' and 'strong' is reached at the expense of their having largely to deny their softer, sensitive feelings. They become closed off from an awareness of this aspect of themselves. This inability in so many men, to value emotional interaction, makes it hard for them to talk about their feelings. It lies at the core of so many dissatisfactions that women feel in heterosexual relationships, and can produce deep levels of loneliness in women unable to share their feelings with male partners.

In families where the father plays a small part, or dies when his son is still young, the boy often has great difficulty in separating from his mother and feeling able to 'explore' the world effectively. The insidious hold a mother can have over a son can be just as crippling as the violent, but often hidden 'hold' an incestuous father has over his daughter. Both are deeply damaging to the child's ability to build a good evaluation of themselves. Such experiences make it very hard for people to separate sufficiently to fully determine how they would like to be.

Apart from the conflicts in our patriarchal society that come from the differences due to the valuing of males over females, there are other powerful differences of race, class, age, education and wealth. Horrifically oppressive experiences occur under widely differing regimes. Political oppression, as well as extremes of wealth and poverty, occur worldwide. A massive change in value judgements is needed to bring about a more equable way of sharing the worlds' goods. Although enough food is produced in the world for every human being not to go hungry, there is no substantial move by wealthy nations to see that this is secured.

There is so much evidence available now that confirms how deeply we all need positive, loving and affirming relationships at all stages of our lives to fulfil our potential. In spite of this our institutions only give scant attention to it. The subject of good relating or parenting plays a minor part in our schools; hospitals and establishments for the elderly tend to infantilise the people who stay in them. There is an enormous task ahead to shift attitudes towards properly valuing the emotional needs of us all.

**Striving towards a value for equality**

Therapy, at its best, offers people an opportunity to re-evaluate themselves within a framework of equality. The work that is undertaken in therapy consists of struggling to understand the conflicting forces operating inside ourselves, as well as questioning and challenging the forces operating in the world outside. This work can best be done within a reliable relationship, where the client feels fully respected and appreciated by the therapist. This form of loving, that should be available in therapy, continually strives towards recognising and accepting the value of equality. It is based on an ideology to do with deeply valuing *all* human beings, regardless of their behaviour, because it strives to understand the reasons for it. This ideology is viewed as subversive to the establishment, because it so strongly challenges the currently held ideologies based on seeking power – the idealising of war and the savouring of the spoils of exploitation. These are largely male ideologies, which so far have dominated the world and now threaten its very existence. We have the examples in history of men from Jesus and Ghandi, to Martin Luther King and Lennon, who have dared not just to preach love and equality, but to live by it and to challenge hierarchical ways of relating. These men have faced violent deaths because the values of loving and preaching peace are viewed as dangerously subversive in our power-structured society.

As Marilyn French writes in her book 'Beyond Power' (1986), perhaps our hope of human beings developing in a new way in the future lies with women the world over, as they have increasing access to education and knowledge even though so much of this holds a huge male bias. It has now become imperative for women to move into public life *differently* from the model that men have so far created, where power and hierarchical ways of relating have led to such fearful levels of distress and violence, all of which stem from fear.

As men in turn become more intimately involved in the private and domestic spheres of life (even in such small ways as being present at the birth of their babies), so it will become harder for them to deny the value of emotions and the need for them to share in the responsibility for good nurturing. When men join women in the struggle for greater equality, this gives men and women the experience of relating to each other in a new, non-hierarchical and vastly more rewarding way.

Can we dare to hope that as we work towards understanding our fears and learning how to control them in ourselves as individuals, so we may in time learn to understand and control them between nations?

BORDERS REGIONAL LIBRARY

# Bibliography

Baker Miller, J. (1973) *Psychoanalysis and Women* (Harmondsworth: Penguin).

Baker Miller, J. (1976) *Toward a New Psychology of Women* (Harmondsworth: Penguin).

Baker Miller, J. (1984) 'The Development of Women's Sense of Self', Work in Progress Paper, The Stone Center, Wellesley College, Massachussetts.

Belotti, E. G. (1973) *Little Girls* (London: Writers and Readers).

Berne, E. (1966) *Games People Play* (London: André Deutsch).

Bowlby, J. (1980) *Attachment and Loss* (Harmondsworth: Penguin).

Broverman, I. and D. et al. (1970) 'Sex-role Stereotypes and Clinical Judgements of Mental Health', *Journal of Consulting and Clinical Psychology*, 34: 1–7.

Chernin, K. (1986) *The Hungry Self* (London: Virago).

Eichenbaum, L. and Orbach, S. (1985) *Understanding Women* (Harmondsworth: Penguin).

Ernst, S. and Goodison, L. (1986) *In Our Own Hands* (London: Women's Press).

French, M. (1986) *Beyond Power: Women, Men and Morals* (London: Jonathan Cape).

Freud, S. (1932) *Interpretation of Dreams* (London: Hogarth Press).

Freud, S. (1949) *An Outline of Psychoanalysis* (London: Hogarth Press).

Fromm, E. (1978) *To Have or To Be* (London: Jonathan Cape).

Hite, S. (1976) *The Hite Report* (London: Talmy Franklin).

Kovel, J. (1976) *A Complete Guide to Therapy* (New York: Pantheon).

Kübler Ross, E. (1973) *On Death and Dying* (London: Tavistock).

Malan, D. H. (1979) *Individual Psychotherapy and the Science of Psychodynamics* (London: Butterworth).

Masters, W. H. and Johnson, V. E. (1970) *Human Sexual Inadequacy* (London: J. H. Churchill).

Miller, A. (1983) *The Drama of Being a Child* (London: Virago).

Miller, A. (1987) *For Your Own Good* (London: Virago).

Norwood, R. (1986) *Women Who Love Too Much* (London: Arrow Press).

Spender, D. (1982) *Invisible Women: The Schooling Scandal* (London: Writers and Readers).

Stanworth, M. (1983) *Gender and Schooling* (London: Hutchinson).

Woodward, J. (1981) 'The Diagnosis and Treatment of Psychosomatic Vulvo-Vaginitis', *The Practitioner*, vol. 225: 1673.

Woodward, J. (1987) 'The Bereaved Twin', Proceedings of International Congress of Twin Studies 1986 (AGMG/Twin Research, Rome).

# Index

133